YORK NOTES

PARADISE LOST
BOOKS I AND II

JOHN MILTON

NOTES BY GEOFF RIDDEN

 Longman

York Press

The right of Geoff Ridden to be identified as Author
of this Work has been asserted by him in accordance
with the Copyright, Designs and Patents Act 1988

YORK PRESS
322 Old Brompton Road, London SW5 9JH

PEARSON EDUCATION LIMITED
Edinburgh Gate, Harlow,
Essex CM20 2JE, United Kingdom
Associated companies, branches and representatives throughout the world

First published 2000
This new and fully revised edition first published 2009

10 9 8 7 6 5 4 3 2 1

ISBN 978–1–4082–1730–6

Phototypeset by Chat Noir Design, France
Printed in China

CONTENTS

PART FIVE
BACKGROUND

PART ONE

INTRODUCTION

STUDYING VERSE NARRATIVES

Reading verse narratives and exploring them critically can be approached in a number of ways, but when reading the text for the first time it is a good idea to consider some, or all, of the following:

- **Format and style**: how do verse narratives differ from other genres of text? How are stanzas or other divisions used to reveal information, and how do the characters or voices convey emotion?

- **The writer's perspective**: consider what the writer has to say, how he or she presents a particular view of people, the world, society, ideas, issues, etc. Are, or were, these views controversial?

- **Shape and structure**: explore the relationship between the main narrative and any subsidiary ones. How do these narratives develop through revelation and reflection, conflicts and resolutions?

- **Choice of language**: does the writer choose to write formally or informally? Does he or she use different registers for characters, voices or groups, vary the sound and style, or employ language features such as **imagery** and **dialect**?

- **Verse and metre**: what rhythms and rhymes does the writer use to create pace and interest, convey an atmosphere or achieve an effect?

- **Links and connections**: what other texts does this verse narrative remind you of? Can you see connections between its narrative, main voices, characters and ideas and those of other texts you have studied? Is the poem part of a literary movement or tradition?

- **Your perspective and that of others**: what are your feelings about the verse narrative? Can you relate to the voices, characters, themes and ideas? What do others say about it – for example, critics or other writers?

These York Notes offer an introduction to *Paradise Lost* Books I and II and cannot substitute for close reading of the text and the study of secondary sources.

 QUESTION

Why do you think a writer might choose to employ complex language that requires the reader to go back and read the text more than once?

 CHECK THE BOOK

For more on narrative poems see Michael Meyer, *The Bedford Introduction to Literature*, (Bedford/St Martin's, 2005). Further guidance on the genre (and on other aspects of literary study) can be found in *The Penguin Dictionary of Literary Terms and Literary Theory* (Penguin, 1999) by J. A. Cuddon, and in Martin Gray's *A Dictionary of Literary Terms* (York Handbooks, 1992).

READING *PARADISE LOST* BOOKS I AND II

Paradise Lost was first published as a poem in ten books in 1667, and was revised and re-published in twelve books in 1674. It is one of the most ambitious works in English literature. Its author, John Milton, attempts nothing less than an explanation of one of the key tenets of the Christian Bible: God's purpose in creating humanity, in the person of Adam and Eve, and then allowing them to be tempted and to fall from grace. The epic poem ends with the expulsion of this pair of fallen human beings from Paradise (the Garden of Eden) into the world as we all know it – a place of pain and of death.

In its opening two Books, *Paradise Lost* introduces us not to the humans at the centre of the poem but to Satan and those fallen angels who find themselves with Satan in Hell, having rebelled against God and been thrown out of Heaven. In fact, *Paradise Lost* is based upon two quite distinct biblical narratives. The story of the Creation is drawn by Milton from the early chapters of Genesis, the first book of the Bible. Although these chapters deal with the beginnings of the world, the establishment of Adam and Eve in the Garden of Eden, the temptation by the serpent and the dismissal of Adam and Eve from the Garden, they do not include any reference to Satan by name, or to the fall of the angels. These narratives are taken from Revelation, the final book of the Bible. In *Paradise Lost*, Milton is thus able to bring together the opening and closing sections of the Bible, the text which was central to his beliefs. Moreover, Milton makes the radical choice to begin with his poem with the aftermath of the fall of angels, in effect turning the biblical sequence on its head.

Milton lived through some of the most troubled times in English history. He was born in 1608, five years after James I succeeded Elizabeth as monarch of England: James was already James VI, King of Scotland. By the time of Milton's death in 1674, the country had been through a revolution, which had led to the execution of its king, James's son Charles I, in 1649, and to the only period of republicanism in English history, during which Oliver Cromwell

CHECK THE BOOK

In the Bible, the first three chapters of Genesis and Revelation, Chapter 12, provide the full biblical sources on which *Paradise Lost* is based. Genesis is the first book of the Old Testament, Revelation the last book of the New Testament.

CONTEXT

The monarchy was re-established in 1660, but the effects of the revolution are still evident today; for example, Charles's death continues to be marked in the calendar of the Church of England where he is revered as a Saint and Martyr.

ruled for almost a decade. The monarchy was restored in 1660, despite the best efforts of Milton, among others, to prevent it.

Religion, specifically Christianity, was of great significance in Milton's time. Although the English Revolution was primarily to do with issues of political power and democracy, it was, in large part, a religious revolution, in which the debate centred on the competing claims of Puritans and the Church of England as to which represented true Christianity. The matters of religion and power were intertwined, since the monarchy supported the established Church, and William Laud was, at the same time, Archbishop of Canterbury and Chief Minister to Charles I. This conflict was to lead to civil war and to many people leaving England for America where they hoped to preserve their religious freedom.

Milton not only lived through this time, but was intimately and centrally involved in its politics. He chose not to retire from public life in order to write: from the 1640s he wrote on the religious issues and debates which led up to the Civil War, and after the execution of Charles I, he was engaged to work on behalf of Cromwell's administration. Throughout his adult life, therefore, Milton was a figure involved in controversy (see **Part Five: Background**).

In terms of literary discourse, there are two principal differences between Milton's time and our own. Firstly, at the time when Milton lived, there was still some debate as to the status of English as a serious language in which to write: even when he was employed by Cromwell's administration, Milton still wrote his public documents on behalf of that administration in Latin. In Milton's time, serious writing in English was still a relatively new phenomenon and there was still a case to be made for English poetry in general, and for an English epic in particular. Secondly, in the twenty-first century we are accustomed to regard the novel as the prime mode of serious comment in literature on matters of the day. Writers such as Salman Rushdie and Ian McEwan are in the forefront of such comment. Poetry, on the other hand, is given a very different status. There is still a Poet Laureate, but the holder of that office is expected only to write verse to commemorate events held to be of national significance, such as the death of the Princess

CHECK THE BOOK

The life and times of William Laud (1573–1645) are described succinctly in N. H. Keble's chapter 'Milton and Puritanism' in *A Companion to Milton* (Wiley Blackwell, 2003). See also **Themes: Puritanism and Christianity**.

CHECK THE BOOK

The emigration of Puritans is the basis for Peter Ackroyd's 1996 novel, *Milton in America* (Sinclair-Stevenson) in which he speculates on what might have happened if Milton had made that journey with his fellow Puritans. This novel provides an accessible introduction to some of the religious debates of this period.

of Wales in 1997. In Milton's day, attitudes to prose and poetry were very different, and if he was to be regarded as the greatest writer in his country, Milton had no option but to write in English and to write in verse.

Milton prepared himself thoroughly for this task by following the examples of the great Classical poets and writing short pastoral poems at the beginning of his career. However, it is clear from Milton's own early writings that he had always had it in his mind to write an **epic**, which was considered the greatest of poetic forms, and a genre in which the poet could celebrate the nation. In doing this, he followed the classical models of Homer and Virgil, as well as that of his fellow-countryman, Edmund Spenser, who had begun an epic in praise of Elizabeth I, *The Faerie Queene*, which remained unfinished at his death in 1599.

Spenser's epic raises some interesting comparisons with that of Milton: it is written in English, in praise of the monarchy, and written by a man who was intimately involved in the politics of his day, spending several years of his life in Ireland. Spenser's epic was, thus, a political work (as, arguably, are all epics), promoting the cause of England at a time when Spenser wanted to see the rebellious Irish suppressed. Milton's *Paradise Lost* was also written in English, but was not written in praise of the monarchy: that was not possible for Milton in 1667 when he had spent the greater part of his life attacking it. Instead, Milton writes not of the English nation, but humanity itself, and of God's plan for humanity. He does this in a complex narrative poem in English, and he makes those choices for very particular reasons.

The period immediately preceding the trial and execution of Charles I in 1649 witnessed a change in the way in which literature was regarded. Printed books were still relatively rare and expensive in Milton's lifetime. However, this period saw a great escalation in the publication of short pamphlets and newspapers: these were often scurrilous in nature, as each party sought to demonise its opponents. Milton could, and did, write political prose pamphlets, but he described these himself as the product of his left hand, as work in an inferior genre. This was, in part, because he, like other

CONTEXT

Readers of English literature in the twenty-first century will commonly trace its ancestry back to the Anglo-Saxons. It may be surprising to realise that most of Milton's contemporaries had no knowledge of this heritage. Even among educated readers, few had access to such Anglo-Saxon texts as *Beowulf* until the nineteenth century.

pamphleteers, did not put his name to some of his earliest prose works. Nevertheless, when these first attempts at prose were published, Milton's identity was quickly discovered and he found himself under personal attack from his enemies. This led to him putting into print his first anthology of poems, *Poems 1645*, a collection which included poetry in several different languages with the implicit aim of asserting that Milton was no mere pamphleteer, but a serious writer: a poet. More than twenty years later, having worked in Cromwell's administration and been briefly imprisoned after the Restoration of the monarchy in 1660, Milton was a published poet once again with the publication of *Paradise Lost*: this was a matter of some significance to him and to the cause which he had espoused.

The English Revolution was centred on religion and politics, but debates on these matters came to involve issues to do with the nature of culture. The anti-monarchists, who might be described as the radicals, were united in very little except their hostility to the Crown and to the Church of England. The writings in support of this viewpoint often took the form of pamphlets, intended for quick circulation and not for posterity. The monarchists, on the other hand, had a more homogeneous view of the world, which included a view of what constituted culture. For them, the monarchy meant high culture, and its supporters included well-known poets, not anonymous pamphleteers: this group has since become known as the Cavalier Poets, and their writing found its way into that still exclusive realm of published work.

It can be argued that, in writing *Paradise Lost*, Milton was attempting to regain the cultural high ground which the monarchists seemed to have under their control. His **epic** poem was a demonstration that it was possible for a writer who was not of the establishment to produce a significant product of high culture.

Generations of readers of *Paradise Lost*, especially those from the late eighteenth century onwards, have found the presentation of these fallen angels, and of Satan in particular, intriguing, fascinating and dangerously alluring. His arguments justifying his rebellion seem at times very convincing, as do his attempts to maintain that

 CHECK THE BOOK

Anthologies, such as those by Erskine-Hill and Storey (Cambridge University Press, 1983), have brought back into print examples from radical prose pamphlets that had long been unavailable. However, the works of the Cavalier Poets did not suffer this obscurity, partly because their poems came from the Establishment and were not regarded as political.

 CHECK THE NET

The works of the Cavalier Poets are discussed on the Luminarium website – **www.luminarium. org**. Click on 'Seventeenth Century English Literature' and then the 'Cavalier Poets'.

CHECK THE BOOK

In the second edition of the poem, published in 1674, Milton provided his readers with a brief summary (which he called 'Argument') at the beginning of each of the twelve Books of *Paradise Lost*. These allow his readers to gain an overall sense of the total narrative in the words of the poet himself. These arguments are reprinted in the Broadbent edition of *Paradise Lost* used in the preparation of these Notes (see **Part Two: Note on the text**).

CHECK THE NET

The Milton List can be found at **http://facultystaff. richmond.edu/ ~creamer/milton**

he and his fellow rebels are actually better off in Hell than they were in Heaven. This raises a range of questions in the minds of readers, such as how can a creature so evidently wicked as Satan be provided by the poet with such powerful arguments? Are we meant to admire Satan? What does the portrayal of Satan contribute to our sense of how we define a hero? Do we find rebellion more exciting than conformity? Later sections of these Notes address the influence of Milton's Satan on the Gothic tradition, and the fascination that the presentation of Satan has had for generations of readers (see **Part Four: Critical history** and **Part Five: Literary background**).

Many questions about the poem can be fully answered only with reference to the whole work – the more you know of the later Books of the poem, the more you will appreciate what Milton is establishing in these opening two sections. If you intend to undertake any further reading on *Paradise Lost*, you will certainly need a sense of the poem as a whole, because, as indicated below, very few critics will limit themselves to discussing only the opening two Books. See **Part Two** for a synopsis of the whole of *Paradise Lost*, and for guidance on how to find and use Milton's 'Arguments'.

Some would claim that Milton has become unfashionable – certainly, Milton is taught much less frequently now in comparison with, for example, Shakespeare (later parts of these Notes investigate in more detail the comparison between these two giants of English Literature). Nevertheless, there are many supporters and advocates of Milton who strive to keep his work on the syllabus and alive in the minds of students. The anniversary of his birth in 2008 saw the publication of new biographies, and of a new *Milton Encyclopedia*. For an indication of the passion of these devotees, one needs to look no further than the website for the Milton List at Richmond University in the USA. Here you will find not only queries and requests about Milton's life and works from scholars all over the world, but also discussions on how to promote Milton's poetry to a new generation of students. Further books and online resources are listed later in **Part Five: Further reading**.

As an illustration of the fact that Milton's work still continues to influence contemporary popular culture, one might note the number of different works from recent years, in print and on film, which are indebted to *Paradise Lost*. These include not only such novels as William Golding's *Lord of the Flies* (1954), now a classic in its own right, but Philip Pullman's trilogy for children *His Dark Materials*, launched with the 1995 novel *Northern Lights*. This ambitious project attempts to rework *Paradise Lost* for teenagers; the first volume cites Book II on its opening page, from which it draws its title.

Perhaps more striking is the opening section of Sadie Plant's book *Zeros and Noughts: Digital Women and the New Technoculture* (Fourth Estate, 1997). These pages, in a book on the digital revolution of the information age, are a reworking of a creation myth, which is considerably indebted to Milton in its insistence on the inevitability of the fall.

There are particular reasons why Milton may suffer in comparison to Shakespeare, and some of these are outlined later in this book, but the study of Milton will survive, not least because of the number of enthusiasts who look for new ways of promoting this study. For example, whilst interest in Shakespeare has been helped by the **parodic**, abridged version of his plays performed by the Reduced Shakespeare Company, there is a 'Reduced Milton' of a very different order produced by the scholar John Hale. He wrote an abridged version of *Paradise Lost* for his students in New Zealand, which he called '*Paradise Lost* Post-haste. John Milton's Epic Poem in Twelve Books Distilled into Twelve Minutes for Educational Purposes'. The London-based Headlong Theatre company did a production of *Paradise Lost*, which toured the country in 2006, adapted by Rupert Goold and Ben Power.

Professor Hale's 'Reduced Milton' is not parodic, unlike the abridged version of Shakespeare. It does, however, remind us, first, that one way to get to know the poem very well is to try to rewrite it, and second, that Milton originally planned this **epic** poem as a drama.

CHECK THE FILM

The first film based on Pullman's work, *The Golden Compass* (the US title for the first book in the series of novels) was directed in 2007 by Chris Weitz.

CHECK THE NET

John Hale's text is available at **www.otago.ac.nz** – search for '12 minute Milton'.

CHECK THE FILM

Milton is not the only writer to present his readers with visions of Satan-like figures, who are fascinating and once were forces for good, or with visions of underworlds. *The Lord of the Rings* trilogy (1954–5) by J. R. R. Tolkien includes the figure of Sauron, whilst the 2006 film *Pan's Labyrinth* (directed by Guillermo del Toro) combines the representation of an invented and fabulous world with real political concerns (the repressions of Franco's Spain after the Second World War).

At the very close of *Paradise Lost*, Adam and Eve, having been expelled from Eden, find that the world is all before them. As you embark on your study of the opening books of the poem, much lies before you too. There are detailed and splendid descriptions, such as that of the fallen angels raising their standard (Book I: 531–49). Moreover, Milton rises to the challenge of describing what might seem to be impossible – Hell itself, a place of strange paradoxes (burning lakes and visible darkness). Milton is even able to imagine what it might be like for the fallen angels, and, most of all, he presents Satan, a fascinating, corrupt, central character. New readers need to pay careful attention to the choices which Milton makes in these opening books – these are crucial to an understanding of just how Satan is able to manipulate his followers, and of Milton and his great **epic** as a whole.

PART TWO

THE TEXT

NOTE ON THE TEXT

Little is known about the composition of *Paradise Lost*. We cannot even be sure whether John Milton wrote the epic sequentially from beginning to end, or whether he had already completed what are now the central Books before composing the description of the fallen angels in Hell. One of Milton's early biographers, his nephew Edward Phillips, claims to have seen a speech by Satan (now Book IV: 32–41) some years before the publication of *Paradise Lost*. He asserts that it was intended by Milton to comprise part of a tragic drama, and there is a manuscript extant, containing drafts for such a tragedy, which probably dates from 1640. Nevertheless, the details of the process of composition of this great poem remain a matter for speculation. This is all the more unusual in that the greater part of the composition of *Paradise Lost* must have taken place after Milton became totally blind (see **Background: Milton's life and works**) and would therefore have involved his dictating passages to a number of amanuenses (people who wrote down his poetry as he dictated it). However, none of these amanuenses left any details as to which passages were dictated or in what order.

The principal sources for the poem can all be found in the Bible, and Milton may also have had access to the tragedy *Adamus Exul* (1601) by Hugh Grotius, whom Milton met in Paris in 1638. More intriguing is the possibility that Milton also had access to the text of an Anglo-Saxon poem, now known as *Genesis B*. This poem occurs in a manuscript now in the Bodleian Library in Oxford, given in about 1651 to Franciscus Junius (1589–1677), a biblical translator and a scholar of Old English. In 1653 he published a transcript of the text in Amsterdam, and there has been speculation that Milton saw this poem: he and Junius were acquainted in the early 1640s. There are certainly similarities between the Anglo-Saxon poem and the opening two Books of *Paradise Lost*, as is confirmed in this extract from *A Milton Encyclopedia* (Associated University Press, 1978), vol. 1, p. 52:

CONTEXT

There has been much debate as to the extent of Milton's knowledge of Anglo-Saxon and his acquaintance with Junius. What is fascinating is that *Genesis B* includes the same causal relationship as *Paradise Lost* does between the fall of the angels and the fall of mankind.

Like Milton's Satan, the Anglo-Saxon Satan is still defiant. He stands on his 'injur'd merit' and claims that his punishment is unjust. Although chained hand and foot ... he is still 'Vaunting aloud' ... In contemplating the temptation of Man, he is clearly motivated by ... envy, yet he takes equal pleasure in the prospect of angering God and perverting His plans ... In such respects *Genesis B* is closer to *Paradise Lost* than any other literary analogue adduced to date.

Paradise Lost was first published in 1667 as an **epic** in ten Books, and shows evidence of having been carefully checked by its author, despite his blindness. After the first three issues of this edition, some preliminary material was added. This included a statement from the printer (Samuel Simmons) to the reader; the Argument (Milton's prose summary of the narrative line of the epic); and an explanation by the poet of his decision to use **blank verse** rather than rhyme.

CHECK THE NET

The online edition of *Paradise Lost* at **www.dartmouth. edu** includes all the Arguments and the Introductory material. Go to the university homepage and search for 'Milton reading room' for online editions of his major works, including *Paradise Lost.*

A second edition appeared a few months before Milton's death in 1674, and this has come to be regarded as the definitive text for modern editions. It includes poems by Samuel Barrow (1625–82) and by Andrew Marvell (1621–78) in praise of *Paradise Lost,* and it redistributes the epic into twelve Books, with the Argument split into twelve sections to precede each individual Book.

These Notes are based upon the 1674 text of Books I and II in *John Milton Paradise Lost Books I–II*, edited by John Broadbent (Cambridge University Press, 1972). References to other Books of *Paradise Lost* are to the version of the 1674 text in Gordon Campbell's edition of *John Milton, Complete English Poems, Of Education, Areopagitica* (Everyman, 1990), which also includes a detailed discussion of Milton's spelling and punctuation. Broadbent's edition includes the Arguments for Books I and II in separate sections in his Introduction.

SYNOPSIS

At the outset of the opening Book of *Paradise Lost*, Milton states that his general purpose is to tell the story of the fall of mankind, through the failure of Eve and Adam to obey the command not to eat the fruit of the forbidden tree, the tree of knowledge. However, he does not begin to relate the events leading up to this fall, and its consequences, until much later in his epic. After the initial statement of intent, Book I takes up the story of a different fall. It describes the rebel angels, newly arrived in Hell, after their own fall which followed their decision to rebel against God and to provoke a war in Heaven, a war which the rebel angels lost. All of this takes place a long time before the fall of mankind, but it is Milton's objective to make the fall of mankind a consequence of the fall of the angels: the rebel angels start a war in Heaven which they lose; they are cast into Hell from where they plot the fall of mankind. That plot is the basis for the opening two Books of *Paradise Lost*.

In Book I the situation of the fallen angels is described, along with the individual characters of their most significant members and their occupations. In Book II they meet in council to decide what is to be done. Finally, it is agreed that Satan will fly off to the new world of man (the term 'man' is used by Milton to refer to humankind in general) to see if he can strike at God through this new creation. Satan's escape from Hell, his meeting with Sin and Death, and his perilous passage to the surface of our world, are all described in Book II.

In Book III the scene switches to Heaven, where God delivers a long speech on the freedom of man to choose between good and evil. At the end of this speech, which foreshadows man's freely chosen disobedience and fall, the Son (Christ) offers himself as the ransom for mankind and God accepts his sacrifice. Meanwhile, Satan has landed on the rim of the universe, and, finding his way in, flies down to the sun and thence to Earth. In Book IV he observes the marital happiness of Adam and Eve and is aroused to a fury of envy, which he expresses in the form of a **soliloquy**: for the first time the reader gains direct access to Satan's thoughts. One of the angels observes his behaviour and reports back to Heaven, causing God to send Gabriel and an angelic patrol to Eden. Satan is thus frustrated in his first attempt to tempt Eve by means of a dream, and he is expelled from Eden.

CHECK THE POEM
You will find much of interest in Milton's early short poem 'On the Morning of Christ's Nativity', which includes a catalogue of false gods similar to that in Book I of *Paradise Lost*.

In Book V, God send his angel Raphael to talk to Adam in Paradise, to warn him of the threat to Eden and, at Adam's request, to tell him of the war in Heaven. The account of the war continues in detail in Book VI, and the conversation between Adam and Raphael goes on in Book VII as the angel responds to Adam's request to know about the creation of the new world of Eden. Book VIII is taken up with Adam telling Raphael what he remembers of his own creation, the creation of Eve and his first meeting with her.

Thus some four books of the epic are taken up with the warning visit from Raphael. The warning is in vain, however, as God had foreknown it would be, and in Book IX Milton changes his tone to one of tragedy, claiming nevertheless that his theme is more truly **heroic** than the stories of Classical and Romantic **epics**. Satan succeeds in his design of persuading Eve to taste the forbidden fruit, and Adam also eats, determined to share Eve's fate 'not deceived, but fondly overcome by female charm'. They become wild, first through lust and then through anger, blaming each other bitterly.

Book X is a tale of retribution and reconciliation. The Son (Christ) descends to Eden to pronounce God's sentence of expulsion, toil and mortality, tempered by the promise of ultimate victory over evil. Adam and Eve are reconciled and accept their fate with resignation. Satan, meanwhile, has not gone unpunished. Returning to Hell in triumph, he is greeted by a universal hiss instead of the expected acclamation; for all his followers have become serpents, and he himself is forthwith transformed into the greatest serpent of them all.

The two concluding Books of *Paradise Lost*, which were originally composed as a single entity, conform to another epic tradition, that of looking into the future. Just as Aeneas was permitted to foresee the Empire of Augustus (27 BC–AD 14) in the *Aeneid*, so Adam is shown a synopsis of Jewish history down to the redemption of mankind by Christ on the Cross. Reconciled to his fate by the promise of ultimate redemption coming after so much evil, Adam takes Eve by the hand as they pass out of Eden to face the hardships of the outside world together.

CONTEXT

The *Aeneid* is an epic poem composed by the Latin poet Virgil in 29BC. Its twelve books tell the story of Aeneas as he journeys from his home in Troy to Italy, and of the war between the Trojans and other nations and states.

 CHECK THE NET

John Dryden's 1697 translation of the *Aeneid* is available online at **http://classics.mit. edu** – click on 'Browse and Comment' and find Virgil in the alphabetical list of authors.

DETAILED SUMMARIES

BOOK I

Book I is made up of five distinct sections:

- An introduction to the epic poem, outlining its intended purpose.
- An introduction to Satan and Beëlzebub, principal among the fallen angels.
- Satan's rallying of the other fallen angels.
- Satan's triumphant speech.
- The building of Pandemonium.

LINES 1–26 – INTRODUCTION TO THE POEM

- Milton establishes the style and the purpose of his epic, which he expects to be the major work of his poetic career.
- He calls for divine inspiration, a way of dedicating his poem to God.

The style is established from the outset as lofty and magnificent. The opening sentence, which in many editions of the poem occupies a full sixteen lines, defines the scope of the poem as extending from the fall of man to the salvation of all mankind through Jesus Christ and also places its author alongside Moses and the greatest of Greek poets. Milton's ambition is, quite simply, to do what has never before been done with poetry: a truly breathtaking claim to make for any work of literature.

COMMENTARY

In some respects, the opening sentence of the poem is misleading, because the subject matter of *Paradise Lost* is not bounded by the fall on the one hand and Christ's crucifixion on the other. The poet

CONTEXT

Moses is one of the most important prophets in Judaism, the faith of the Jewish people, and also an important prophet in many other faiths, including Christianity. His story is contained in the book of Exodus, the second book of the Old Testament section of the Bible. He is commanded by God to lead the Hebrews out of slavery in Egypt. For forty years they wander in the desert, and, during that time, Moses receives the Ten Commandments, which are the cornerstones for guiding human behaviour in both Judaism and Christianity.

is about to describe a narrative that precedes the fall, and will go on to describe the war in Heaven, an even earlier episode. His poem will end not with the anticipation of the life, ministry and death of Christ, but includes a description of the state of the Church in Milton's own time, through the voice of Michael, the angel sent by God in the final books of *Paradise Lost* to expel Adam and Eve from Eden, and also the leader of God's army against Satan's rebels.

The opening line of this **epic** poem is, in itself, a striking instance of poetic ambiguity. Milton tempts the reader into believing that the break at the end of the line – the completion of the ten syllables characteristic of **blank verse** – is also a break in meaning. In other words, that the first line represents a complete sentence: 'Of man's first disobedience, and the fruit'. In that interpretation, we might expect *Paradise Lost* to be concerned with the first disobedience of mankind and the fruit of that disobedience. Milton, however, runs the line on so that the fruit is not the consequence of the disobedience, but the fruit of the forbidden tree. Of course, the 'fruit' is, in fact, both the outcome of the sin of disobedience and the literal fruit on the tree. Milton specifically refers to an apple only once in *Paradise Lost,* when Satan, returning to Hell after corrupting Eve and Adam, describes what he has done in these terms (Book X: 485–7):

> Him by fraud I have seduced
> From his creator, and the more to increase
> Your wonder, with an apple . . .

Milton's punctuation can be confusing for a modern reader, since it is primarily designed to indicate pauses and rhythms rather than to indicate grammatical structures. It also therefore poses a challenge to any editor of Milton's poetry. Milton had his own system of punctuation, and editors have always had to decide whether to change it to fit with contemporary conventions or to leave it as Milton intended. Mindele Treip wrote an entire book on the subject (*Milton's Punctuation and Changing English Usage, 1582–1676*, Methuen, 1970) in which she says that Milton's punctuation 'tunes our ear to have further expectations beyond those of grammar' (p. 114).

 CHECK THE BOOK

The subject of Milton's punctuation is widely discussed in other books: David Scott Kastan, in his edition of *Paradise Lost* (Hackett, 2005), says in the 'Textual Introduction' that 'Milton's punctuation . . . is designed more for the ear than for the mind, more to allow the rhythm to be experienced by the reader' (p. lxxiii). See also W. B. Hunter and J. T. Shawcross (eds), *Milton's English Poetry: Being Entries from a Milton Encyclopedia* (Bucknell University Press, 1986), p.109.

In the opening lines of Book I Milton seeks inspiration from the Holy Spirit ('Heavenly Muse', 6), which was present at creation (19–20), according to the biblical accounts in Genesis and the Gospel of John. In doing this, although the poem may appear to begin with the fallen angels in Hell and therefore not to mirror the beginning of the Old Testament section of the Bible, Milton contrives to refer to the opening of Genesis, and to include numerous references to Exodus, the second book of the Bible and to other books from the Old Testament.

In one sense this search for inspiration makes Milton not responsible for his epic: he is simply the mouthpiece for God, rather as the American novelist Harriet Beecher Stowe (1811–96) could claim that she did not write *Uncle Tom's Cabin*, but merely took God's dictation. Milton is thus claiming his own private divine inspiration. There is no doubt, however, that Milton was very aware of his place as author of this epic, even if, as recent critics have noted (see **Critical perspectives: Critical history**), *Paradise Lost*, like *Uncle Tom's Cabin*, is also the product of a specific historical moment at which it was written.

> **CONTEXT**
>
> The Holy Spirit is part of the divine Trinity – and is identified as 'the Word' in the opening verses of the Gospel of John and has also been described as the inspiration for all prophets. Milton thus places himself in this prophetic line.

> **CONTEXT**
>
> Harriet Beecher Stowe's novel *Uncle Tom's Cabin* was published in 1852. In it, Stowe attacked the institution of slavery in the USA and her book helped to intensify and polarise the conflict between supporters and opponents of slavery. This conflict eventually led to the Civil War in the USA.

GLOSSARY

1	**first**	this word is repeated throughout the early section of this Book (for example lines 19, 27, 28 and 33), emphasising that this is the beginning of Milton's epic
2	**mortal taste**	deadly taste, but also tasting by a human being
6–7	**secret top / Of Oreb, or of Sinai**	the holy mountains named in the Old Testament book of Exodus, frequently referred to in this opening Book of *Paradise Lost*
10	**Sion**	a hill in Jerusalem
11	**Siloa's brook**	a pool in Jerusalem
15	**Aónian**	the mountain believed to be the home of the Greek poetic muses
17–8	**that dost prefer / Before all temples**	a reference to Christ's condemnation of the misuse of the temple, but also an indication of Milton's Puritan nonconformity (see **Background: Milton's life and works**)

LINES 27–298 – INTRODUCTION TO SATAN AND BEËLZEBUB

- Milton introduces the principals among the fallen angels: Satan, and his close ally Beëlzebub.
- Satan and Beëlzebub have their first exchange in Hell.

Milton describes Satan in detail, and then begins the process of describing Hell, a complex location in which the fallen angels strive to find some stability.

In this section, Milton includes a summary in lines 34–49 of what is to be the central action of the whole poem. This traces the career of Satan back from the deception of Eve, described at the end of the poem, to the revolt in Heaven, which has taken place just before the epic begins.

 QUESTION

Why is Beëlzebub so crucial to the opening Books of *Paradise Lost*, and why do you think he does not appear again?

He details the fall of the angels who rebelled with Satan (50–83) and then concentrates on the first speeches of Satan (84–124) and of Beëlzebub (128–55). Satan's reply (156–91) reveals his true motive, which is always to do what is evil.

Milton then describes Satan in terms of superlatives, emphasising his size and his majesty (192–241), and this description continues at line 295. The plight of Satan is also given here, and his intention to make himself ruler of Hell. After a brief response from Beëlzebub, which completes their initial debate, Satan and Beëlzebub make their first moves in surveying Hell (242–98).

COMMENTARY

In Satan's opening speech, his account of the war in Heaven is crucially biased: we could easily believe from his words that all the angels had rebelled. Beëlzebub is allowed only a much shorter speech, and one which illustrates his uncertainty. He is unsure whether angels can, in fact, perish, and this leads him to the dreadful possibility that the fallen angels, now recovering their strength, may be condemned to everlasting servitude:

> what if he our Conqueror . . .
> Have left us this our spirit and strength entire
> Strongly to suffer and support our pains (143–7)

Satan is subtle, too, in his argument. For example in lines 93–4 he argues that the knowledge of the angels was limited by God: they had no idea of the extent of God's power. Satan uses this alleged limitation as an excuse for rebellion, arguing that the actions of the fallen angels were born of a desire to discover how powerful God was. This prefigures the fall of mankind, which stems from a similar desire to discover forbidden knowledge.

The comment by the poet in line 126 that Satan is 'Vaunting aloud, but racked with deep despair' encapsulates the paradox of Satan's situation: outwardly he boasts confidently, but inwardly he is in turmoil.

In his speech from lines 156–91, Satan seems almost to acknowledge the infinite goodness of God, by recognising the possibility that God might seek to bring forth goodness even from the evil of the fallen angels. This idea that a fall may be fortunate becomes more significant in relation to the fall of mankind, especially in the final Books of *Paradise Lost* (see **Critical perspectives: Critical history**).

This idea is continued at lines 210–20: 'nor ever thence ... poured', where Milton, through the voice of the **narrator**, makes it clear that any action which Satan takes can be taken only with God's permission, and that whatever evil Satan may commit will bring only infinite goodness, grace and mercy from God. The concepts of goodness, grace and mercy are more fully developed and defined in Book III.

Despite this inner turmoil Satan seems to believe that he himself can effect a kind of creation: not the creation of worlds or beings which God can bring about, but the use of his mind to render his physical state either better or worse: 'The mind is its own place' (254). Gordon Campbell suggests that this is a heretical view (*John Milton, Complete English Poems, Of Education, Areopagitica*, Everyman, 1990, p. 156) based on the opinions of Amalric, a

CHECK THE BOOK
Book XII contains the dialogue between Adam and the Archangel Michael, in which Michael reveals the consequences of the fall of mankind. Look particularly at lines 469–78.

The idea that Hell is a state of mind rather than a physical location is also expressed by the character Mephistopheles in Christopher Marlowe's play *Doctor Faustus* (1604), for example: 'Why, this is Hell, nor am I out of it' (Act I Scene 3); and 'Hell hath no limits nor is circumscribed/ In one self place, where we are is Hell' (Act II Scene 1).

twelfth-century French philosopher who argued that Heaven and Hell were states determined simply through one's conscience. However, a comparable sentiment is expressed by Milton's near contemporary, John Donne, in his love poem 'The Good Morrow' (1633): 'For love, all love of other sights controls, / And makes one little room, an everywhere.'

Satan appears to believe that distance from God will bring freedom to the fallen angels (see 258–9). This is a belief which was paralleled in the thinking of many of those Protestants who fled Europe for the New World in Milton's time: they expected to find freedom from religious oppression (see also **Background: Historical background**). Milton fashions, through Satan, an inversion of his own sympathetic view of these exiles, as expressed in this sentence from his first prose pamphlet: 'what numbers of faithful and freeborn Englishmen, and good Christians, have been constrained to forsake their dearest home whom nothing but the wide ocean, and savage deserts of America, could hide and shelter from the fury of the bishops?' (*Of Reformation*, 1641, in *Milton's Prose Writings*, ed. K. M. Burton, Everyman, 1958, p. 34).

The description of Satan emphasises that he remains a magnificent and fearsome figure. His shield is the size of the moon, and his size is compared with that of mythical giants. Although he is an angel, he is described in human terms, in that he walks (295). However, some of the imagery used to describe Satan is very telling in undercutting his argument, and his impressiveness. For example, the comparison with Leviathan (201) is a particularly appropriate point of comparison, not least because Leviathan is a sea creature, and Hell has been described thus far as a watery region. Moreover, he provides an illusion of stability, such that some fishermen mistake him for a rock and try to anchor on his back, believing themselves to be in a place of safety. Likewise, Satan seems to offer security to those who trust in him, a security which is equally illusory.

The second figure introduced in this section is Beëlzebub. He is described on several occasions in the New Testament as the prince of demons, for example, in Mark 3:22: 'The scribes who had come from Jerusalem said, "He is possessed by Beëlzebub" and "By the prince of demons he drives out demons".' Although he is a prominent character in the opening two Books, Beëlzebub does not appear in the rest of the poem.

GLOSSARY

28	**what cause** Milton is constantly looking for causes and logical explanations throughout his epic
30	**Favoured of** this is ambiguous: 'favoured of' means both 'honoured by' and 'resembling'
	fall the opening two Books include many references to falling and to rising (see, for example, Book I: 330–4)
34	**infernal serpent** Satan
40	**equalled the most High** this is, effectively, a **paradox**, since it is in this sense impossible to equal the highest
44	**vain attempt** this means both 'attempt which was in vain' and 'attempt prompted by vanity'
48	**adamantine** unbreakable
59	**as far as angels' ken** as far as angels can see
64	**discover** make visible
70–1	**Such place … rebellious** these lines raise fundamental issues about knowledge and creation – it appears that Hell was always there, waiting for occupants, but the angels did not know of it
74	**from the centre … to the utmost pole** from the equator to the pole
80	**Palestine** Beëlzebub is first associated with the Philistines (who lived in ancient Palestine) in II Kings 1
87	**Myriads** countless numbers
104	**dubious battle** a battle in which the likely outcome is unclear; in fact, there could never be any doubt about the result of this battle
105	**field** battle
111	**bow and sue for grace** these are cornerstones of Christian religious practice
125	**apostate** one who has abandoned or renounced his or her religion
133	**Whether upheld by strength, or chance, or fate** Beëlzebub cannot concede that the power of God might be God's by right – in his view it must be a matter of chance

continued

CONTEXT

Milton suggests here (80–1), and elsewhere in these opening Books, that the fallen angels received their names at later points in human history (see the list at lines 392 ff.). Satan seems to be the only one of the fallen angels whose name is given in Heaven, changed from his earlier name of Lucifer after his rebellion.

CONTEXT

At lines 196–208 the comparison, 'in bulk as huge … morn delays', gives us the first instance in *Paradise Lost* of one of the most famous features of the poem: the **epic simile**. This extended comparison, more than a dozen lines in length, allows Milton to place his poem in the ranks of the great epics of the past as he compares the size of Satan with monsters from classical tradition.

169–71	**But see … Heaven** this is, arguably, the first event in the poem, as Satan witnesses the end of the attack from Heaven. He attributes this either to God's scorn, or to the end of God's appetite for war
178	**slip the occasion** lose the opportunity (but the root of 'occasion' in Latin means 'fall')
184	**the tossing of these fiery waves** we are reminded that Hell is an unstable place (see **Themes: Uncertainty and instability** and **Extended commentaries – Text 1**)
196	**rood** a unit of area, usually a quarter of an acre
199	**Briáreos or Typhon** giants of classical legend (see also Book II: 539)
232–3	**Pelorus and Ætna** a promontory (modern-day Cape Faro) and a volcano in Sicily
239	**Stygian** dark; the adjective derives from Styx, the river of the underworld in Greek mythology
240–1	**by their … Power** compare with lines 210–20
246	**now is sovereign** Satan cannot see that God's sovereignty is not a temporary state – God is always sovereign and always has been, not just 'now'
248	**force hath made supreme** here Satan seems to believe, as Beëlzebub suggested earlier (133), that God has achieved victory simply through superior strength
252	**new possessor** Satan argues that, because he occupies Hell, he therefore possesses it. This is a faulty argument, but a popular view, which has often been deployed by colonising powers throughout human history
263	**Better to reign in Hell, than serve in Heaven** in this single **epigrammatic** line, Satan summarises his entire ambition
266	**astonished** stunned
268	**unhappy mansion** possibly 'unhappy state of being' rather than 'mansion' in its current sense of 'magnificent building'. Since nothing has yet been built in Hell, Milton would be unlikely to use the latter meaning
274	**If once they hear that voice** Beëlzebub shrewdly draws attention to the heart of Satan's power: his voice. Satan is a master of **rhetoric**
282	**pernicious highth** either a height which could have been fatal, or a height which was wicked. Beëlzebub could perhaps be suggesting that Heaven was itself wicked

CONTEXT

At line 266, Milton makes reference to an 'oblivious pool'. This is a pool which has the property of making all who drink its waters forget their past. Milton returns to this idea in Book I: 301, where the fallen angels 'lay entranced', and, more specifically, in Book II: 583, where he describes the Greek myth of the River Lethe, from which he derives the notion of waters of forgetfulness.

285	**Ethereal temper** tempered (i.e. created) in Heaven
287–91	**like the moon … globe** a further **epic simile** based upon the 'Tuscan artist', the astronomer Galileo, whom Milton met on his European tour (see **Background: Milton's life and works**)
289	**Fésolè** the name of the range of hills overlooking Florence, where Galileo was imprisoned
290	**Valdarno** the valley of the River Arno, overlooked by the hills of Fésolè (Fiesole)
290	**descry** discover
291	**spotty** spotted: the surface of the moon would appear to be spotted when seen through a telescope
294	**ammiral** a variant of 'admiral', **synecdoche** for the ship carrying an admiral
	wand the most slender of sticks
296	**marl** clay, soil, earth

CONTEXT

Milton uses the word 'azure' at line 297. It is usually used to refer to the colour blue, but has extended its meaning to the blue of an unclouded sky. Milton is, here, the first writer to use the term to refer to unclouded vaults of Heaven.

LINES 299–587 – SATAN'S RALLYING OF THE OTHER FALLEN ANGELS

- This section begins with a description of the fallen angels.
- Satan begins to rouse them.
- Milton then describes, at length, the reaction of the fallen angels as they respond to Satan's call.

This section develops the comment of Beëlzebub (274) on the power of Satan's rhetoric. The rebel angels are initially described as being 'entranced' and 'abject', but Satan is able to stir them through the force of his persuasive words.

He begins this process by using flattery (as he did in his initial address to Beëlzebub), addressing them with titles of rank. He suggests two very different reasons why they might be lying here: the worthy reason of resting after battle, or the very unworthy reason of having admitted defeat.

CONTEXT

Milton makes extensive use of his knowledge of the Old Testament in this section, giving names to the principals among the fallen angels which are derived from those fallen gods named extensively in the early books of the Old Testament and described there as having tried to seduce the chosen people from the true God. For one example, see Joshua 24.

The fallen angels rouse themselves as a result of fear, and their leaders are named and described. Towards the end of this catalogue (506–21), Milton adds a secondary list of false gods, derived from Greek mythology and therefore, as far as Milton is concerned, inferior even to the false gods of the Bible.

COMMENTARY

Milton moves in this section from a dialogue between Satan and Beëlzebub, which is, in some respects, a private scene, to a fully public scene with the other rebel angels. Although the principal emphasis continues to be on Satan, there is also considerable information given on the most significant among the fallen angels (the twelve fallen 'disciples'). The analogy with the disciples of Christ begins with the parody of Luke 22:43–4, which records the failure of the disciples to stay awake after the Last Supper when Christ prayed in Gethsemane, and continues in the full description of these twelve fallen angels in lines 392–505. The classical epics (see **Literary background**) included this kind of lengthy catalogue of names. The list here comprises Moloch (392–405); Chemos (406–18); Baälim and Ashtaroth (419–37); Astoreth (437–46); Thammuz (446–57); Dagon (457–66); Rimmon (467–76); Osiris, Isis and Orus (476–89); and, finally, Belial (490–505).

CONTEXT

Moloch is to feature prominently in the debate at the beginning of Book II. He is referred to as a false god in the Old Testament, in II Kings 23:10. The name 'Moloch' means 'king', and his inclusion is possibly a very subtle piece of satire by Milton against the monarchy. This same chapter in II Kings includes reference to the destruction of temples to other false gods, including Baal: all of this occurs during the reign of Josiah (see *Paradise Lost*, Book I: 418).

GLOSSARY

299	Nathless nevertheless
303	Vallombrosa a valley in Etruria (a region corresponding roughly to modern-day Tuscany)
303	Etrurian shades the woods of Tuscany
304	sedge a rush-like plant which grows in wet places
305	Orion in Greek mythology, a hunter and giant who was turned into a constellation when he died
307	Busiris an Egyptian pharaoh
	Memphian from the Egyptian city of Memphis
309	sojourners of Goshen the Israelites
319	repose restore, regain
322	abject posture posture of surrender
324	Cherub and seraph the first two of the nine theological orders of angels (see **Themes: Leadership and authority**)

325	ensigns the flags hoisted in battle
	till anon until eventually
329	Transfix fasten
332	wont accustomed
335	Nor did they not perceive the evil plight the double negative might lead to the sense being lost here. Milton is saying that the fallen angels were very aware of their situation and their pain, but their fear of Satan made them obey
338–43	Amram's son is an allusion to Moses: one of several references to Exodus in this opening Book. It specifically refers to the plague of locusts he brought on the Egyptians (Exodus 10)
345	cope cloak (specifically, the cloak of a priest) or canopy. The phrase 'under the cope of Heaven', meaning 'in all the world', was quite common from the fourteenth century to the eighteenth century – here, Milton makes a startling departure from that common phrase
348	sultan leader; in Milton's time the word would also have carried the negative connotations of an Eastern, unchristian tyrant
349	light alight, land
350	brimstone sulphur, a fiery element (see line 69)
351	populous north in ancient times, the threat to Roman civilisation came from the peoples of northern Europe
352	frozen loins a **metaphor** for the cold lands of the north
353	Rhene ... Danaw the Rhine and Danube, rivers which were regarded as protecting Rome, and the Christian world, from the armies of the barbarians
360	erst formerly
362	rased erased, removed
363	books of life the books referred to in Revelation 3:5 and 21:27, which are God's records of those who will escape damnation
364	sons of Eve humanity
366	high sufferance divine permission
372	gay religions full of pomp and gold Milton, like all Puritans, despised religious practices which involved lavish ceremony and decorated churches

continued

CONTEXT

Note that, at line 302, the leaves are described as 'autumnal': this season, was known in Milton's time as 'Fall', as it still is in the USA. In Book IX, Adam weaves a garland of flowers for Eve: when he meets her she tells him that she has eaten of the forbidden tree, and, at once, all the flowers in the garland die off (Book IX: 892 ff.).

CONTEXT

In the Old Testament book of Ezekiel, the prophet is shown women weeping for the god Tammuz (Thammuz) by the gates of the Temple. Thammuz (446) was a Babylonian fertility god, who, according to mythology, was slain by a boar. In ancient Syria, the festival of Tammuz took place in spring when the River Adonis was flooded with red mud, interpreted as the blood of Tammuz and a sign of his re-birth. The combination of Thammuz and Adonis (450) is an indication of the relationship between the mythologies in different cultures, and of Milton's extensive knowledge of them.

373	**devils to adore for deities** to adore devils instead of gods
380	**promiscuous crowd** a crowd unworthy to be named individually
383	**next** next to
386	**Jehovah** the name used for God in the Old Testament
391	**affront** confront
396	**the Ammonite** the tribe of the Ammonites
403	**opprobrious** corrupted
	grove shady wood
405	**type of Hell** image or model of Hell
411	**asphaltic pool** the Dead Sea
413	**Israel** the tribes of the Israelites
418	**Josiah** a King of Judah (Israel) described in II Kings 22–3
423–31	**For spirits … fulfil** the gender of angels and spirits was a matter to which Milton devoted some attention: he returns to it in a discussion between Adam and the angel Raphael at the end of Book VIII
429	**Dilated** expanded
433	**Their living strength** the true God which sustained their lives
	unfrequénted abandoned
441	**Sidonian virgins** virgins from the Phoenician city of Sidon (in modern-day Lebanon)
444	**uxorious** excessively devoted to his wife
455	**Ezekiel** an Old Testament prophet. This incident is related in Ezekiel 8:14–17
456	**alienated** exiled (also, having turned away from God)
	Judah an alternative term for Israel
458	**captive ark** the ark of the covenant captured by the Philistines
460	**grunsel** threshold
469	**lucid** clear and bright
472	**sottish** foolish
477	**crew** rabble
481	**disguised in brutish forms** Milton believes the false gods of the Egyptians (such as Osiris, Isis and Orus) to have the form of animals, rather than having the human shape of the true God

484	**calf in Oreb** the false god worshipped by the Israelites (Exodus 32)
490	**Belial** generally used in the Old Testament to refer to a state of sinfulness. This is why he has no temple (line 492)
495	**Eli's sons** the sons of the priest Eli, whose wickedness is described in I Samuel 2:12–24
497	**In courts and palaces he also reigns** the sense of Belial as representing corruption in general allows Milton to attack courts and the aristocracy
502	**flown** swollen
506–21	**These … isles** Milton is dismissive of these Greek gods, refusing to name them in full detail because their list is so 'long to tell', and because they inhabit several places ('in Crete … or on the Delphian cliff … Or in Dodona')
523	**damp** depressed
524	**Obscure** hidden
527	**he** Satan
	wonted usual, accustomed
528	**recollecting** recovering
529	**Semblance of worth, not substance** the distinction here between 'Semblance' (appearance) and 'substance' (reality) is crucial. Satan's speeches to the fallen angels do not reveal the uncertainty he really feels, nor does his flattery of them reveal the true extent of their misery
533	**standard** military flag
536	**advanced** raised up
537	**meteor** comet
539	**Seraphic** belonging to the seraphs (see 324)
540	**metal** trumpets
546	**orient colours** the bright colours of the east (as at sunrise)
547	**helms** helmets
548	**serried** tightly packed
549	**anon** immediately
550	**phalanx** a military formation
	Dorian mood a simple, solemn style of music
556	**swage** assuage

continued

CONTEXT

In Ovid's *Metamorphoses* 10.150–1, the warfare between the Giants and the gods of Olympus takes place on the Phlegraean plain (see lines 577–9). The son of Oedipus, Polyneices, besieged Thebes, and, in the wars between the Greeks and the Trojans, at the conflict at Ilium (Ilium is another name for Troy) the heroes were assisted by the gods.

 QUESTION

What evidence can you find of flattery and insincerity in Satan's speeches in Books I and II?

CONTEXT

Charlemagne was King of the Franks in the eighth and ninth century. After his death, he became the subject of many legends, and even makes an appearance in Dante's fourteenth century Italian **epic**, the *Divine Comedy*. However, no version of the story of Charlemagne locates his death as happening at Fontarabbia (Fuenterrabia on the Spanish coast). Some commentators suggest that this place name is used by Milton because that is where the future king of England, Charles II, went in 1659 to seek support from the Spanish and the French.

557	touches notes of music
561	charmed possibly not a positive term here, with its connotations of enchantment and magic
563	horrid bristling with spears
564	guise disguise
567	files military divisions
568	travérse across
570	visages faces
571	sums calculates
575–6	that small infantry / Warred on by cranes the small infantry attacked by cranes is an incident in the classical epic the Iliad
579	auxiliar gods assisting the human combatants
580	Uther's son King Arthur, legendary king of the Britons
583–7	Aspramont … Fontarabbia the places named here are all to be found in legends and romances
586	Charlemagne Charles the Great was a real historical figure

LINES 588–669 – SATAN'S TRIUMPHANT SPEECH

- There is a brief introduction to Satan's speech by the narrator.
- The speech itself takes up the remainder of this section.

The **narrator** prefaces Satan's speech with a description designed to indicate the ambiguity of Satan's situation. He is more impressive than the other fallen angels, but his magnificence is now flawed ('ruined', 'obscured', 593–4).

Satan refuses to acknowledge God's divine superiority, describing God as ruling merely through ancient custom (639–40). He goes on to accuse God of being responsible for the fall of the angels: his logic is that God concealed his own power, and therefore tempted the angels to test his might (see 641–2).

The climax of the speech (646–7) is in itself a neat summary of how Satan operates: he has failed to rebel against God through force, and now turns to the disreputable practices of fraud and guile.

COMMENTARY

The voice of the narrator has been present from the very beginning of Book I, and this is a particularly fine example of how Milton uses that voice to influence the reader, even to the extent of including a description of Satan's tearful state as he prepares to address his followers:

> Thrice he essayed, and thrice in spite of scorn,
> Tears such as angels weep, burst forth (619–20)

However, any shred of sympathy we may feel for this emotional Satan is quickly dispelled as he speaks of God so dismissively and arrogantly: the phrase 'Monarch in Heaven' (638) is especially telling and disparaging. The speech also includes the very first reference to the creation of a new place and a new race (Eden and mankind).

CONTEXT

Note that, in line 634, Satan describes the possibility of the fallen angels returning to Heaven by being 'Self-raised', i.e. raised by their own power. It is a favourite ploy of Satan in *Paradise Lost* to claim that he and his followers are capable of action independent of God.

GLOSSARY

588	observed gave honour to
590	eminent tall
593	arch angel principal among the ranks of the angels (see note to Book I:324)
594–9	as when the sun … Darkened so an **epic simile** comparing Satan's appearance in his fallen state to that of the sun when obscured by cloud or in eclipse (see also **Language and style: Images of the sun**)
596	Shorn deprived
603	considerate deliberate
606	The fellows of his crime, the followers rather the fallen angels are not equally to blame: they followed Satan
608	lot share
609	amerced deprived
613	scathed scorched
619	essayed attempted
624	event outcome

continued

632	**puissant** powerful
632–3	**whose exile / Hath emptied Heaven** Satan's account of the war again exaggerates the number of angels who followed him (see 100–5)
637	**he** God
650	**rife** widespread, common
651	**fame** rumour
655	**pry** like 'fraud' and 'guile' (line 646), 'pry' is a loaded term which suggests deviousness – it is hardly the behaviour we expect of an angel
656	**eruption** breaking forth from constraint
660	**despaired** no longer to be hoped for
666	**illumined** gave light to

CONTEXT

The word 'conclave' (795), also meaning a 'secret meeting', usually refers to the assembly which elects a Pope. Thus Milton, through use of this one word, makes Catholicism a product of Hell.

CONTEXT

Mammon is identified in a sermon by Jesus in Matthew 6:19–21, 24) as wealth or riches. The figure also features in Book II of Spenser's *The Faerie Queene*. Mulciber is an alternative name for the Roman god Vulcan, the god of fire.

Lines 670–798 – The building of Pandemonium

- Milton describes how Hell is mined for treasure.
- Those treasures are used by the fallen angels to construct Pandemonium, their palace in Hell.
- The fallen angels enter Pandemonium to begin their 'conclave'.

The treasure of Hell, especially gold, is discovered by the fallen angels, led by Mammon. The process of mining and the preparation of the gold is described in detail. The building constructed from the product of this work is designed by Mulciber, and the heralds of the fallen angels summon their fellow rebels to a meeting in Pandemonium to decide what course of action they should take next.

Commentary

The greater part of Book I so far has been taken up with speeches, but Milton turns here to description, political comment and satire. 'Pandemonium', a word now used in the general sense of a noisy, chaotic place, means 'the place of all demons', and is a word of Milton's own invention. This construction, the first of all buildings, and the first of all objects not created directly by God, is a product of Hell: Milton no doubt wanted his readers to contrast this artificial construction in all its ugliness with the natural beauties of Eden and Heaven.

Through the construction of Pandemonium the fallen angels are no longer 'weltering' (78) in an unstable environment – they have obtained some measure of stability and established a court. However, this apparent move to civilisation cannot be taken at face value, as the **narrator** is at pains to point out. This is the first example in history of the establishing of a court, and it is founded by the fallen angels: the very evident implication is that it, and all subsequent courts, are wicked and to be scorned. This may thus be a reference to the political situation of Milton's own time (see **Historical background** and **Themes: Puritanism and Christianity**).

This section also includes what is a rarity in *Paradise Lost*, a humorous pun. At line 790, Milton uses the expression 'at large' to describe the gathered angels, in two different senses. On the one hand, this means simply 'free to move about', in the sense that an escaped criminal might be described as 'at large'; on the other hand, 'at large' is in ironic contrast to what has happened in the narrative. In order to enter Pandemonium, the fallen angels are forced to reduce their size to their 'smallest forms' (769), and yet are still 'at large': Milton thus undercuts any sense that this is a grand occasion by contriving this joke. As is indicated in the section on **Leadership and control** in Part Three of these Notes, this reduction in size does not affect all the rebels, but only those who are not given names. The chief among the fallen angels retain their size, and from this derive their authority and status. Furthermore, as we learn from the beginning of Book II, Satan sits on a throne at this assembly, elevated above the rest, highest in the hierarchy. This should make us alert to the need to guard against viewing these first two Books as entirely separate entities.

The final word of this first Book is 'began' (798) which may seem an odd term with which to close a Book, were it not for the fact that Milton intends his readers not to stop here, but to carry on.

CHECK THE NET

Using the online version of *Paradise Lost*, check the ways in which Milton ends each of the Books of his poem so as to encourage his readers to want to read the next Book.

GLOSSARY

670	grisly horrible
671	Belched Milton portrays the site of Pandemonium as if it were a disgusting human body
672	scurf thin turf, having the appearance of poor skin
683	aught anything
684	vision beätific the sight of God
687	treasures better hid treasures it would have been preferable not to find
690	ribs of gold Eve is formed from one of Adam's ribs
690–2	Let none … bane Milton, in typical Puritan fashion, despises wealth and splendour: he therefore locates the source of such display in Hell
692	the precious bane the curse of gold: this is an **oxymoron**
694	the works of Memphian kings the Egyptian pyramids
697	reprobate evil
700	Nigh nearby
703	founded melted (as in 'foundry'), but possibly also with the sense here of 'originated'
704	Severing separating
	scummed skimmed, removed the scum
	dross the waste material produced when smelting metal
706	various complicated
711	exhalation breath or vapour
712	dulcet sweet-sounding
713	temple a place of worship of which Milton would have disapproved (see 17–18)
	pilasters rectangular columns
714	Doric the oldest and simplest of the ancient Greek orders of architecture
715	architrave top beam
716	Cornice ornamental moulding
	frieze a decoration between the architrave and the cornice
	bossy rounded
717	fretted elaborately carved

CONTEXT

The story of the building of the Tower of Babel (694) is told in Genesis 11:1–9. The point Milton is making here is that Babel was the product of human pride; it was built as a monument to mankind rather than to the glory of God. Milton here forges a link between the building of Babel and that of Pandemonium.

720	Belus and Serapis Belus is the Babylonian god also known as Bel; Serapis is an Egyptian god
723	straight immediately
724	brazen made of brass
	discover reveal
727	Pendent hanging
728	cressets vessels holding fire for light
729	naphtha an inflammable liquid
	asphaltus black resin
732	his hand Mulciber's handiwork (he is finally identified in line 740)
739	Ausonian land the Greek name for Italy
745	zenith the highest point of Heaven
750	engines skills, wiles
	sent thrown
751	industrious ingenious
753	awful inspiring awe or reverence
758	squarèd regiment troops drawn up in squares
759	By place or choice the worthiest given rank either by appointment or through election
761	Attended accompanied by attendants
764	soldan's sultan's (see also note to line 348)
765	paynim pagan (and therefore, like 'the soldan', not to be admired)
766	career charge
774	expatiate walk about freely
776	straitened confined
780	pygmean the land of the pygmies (hence the adjective 'pygmean') had traditionally been located in India since Roman times
785	arbitress as a judge
787	jocund happy
789	incorporeal having no bodily form
795	close recess secret meeting

CONTEXT

Jove is the Roman name for Zeus, the Greek god who cast Mulciber (or Vulcan) from Heaven. Milton whets our appetite for this story from the *Iliad*, only to declare that it is a lie ('**thus they relate, / Erring**', 746–7). The *Iliad* is, like the *Odyssey*, a Greek epic poem from the nineth century BC, attributed to Homer.

BOOK II

Book II is made up of three distinct sections:

- The great debate itself, which comprises a number of separate speeches.

- The description of the fallen angels after Satan's departure.

- Satan's voyage and his encounters, especially with Sin and Death.

LINES 1–520 – THE GREAT DEBATE

QUESTION

In his concluding speech, Beëlzebub suggests two further reasons for the incursion against mankind (see 390–402). One is that possession of Eden, closer to Heaven, may give the fallen angels a base from which to launch a further attack on Heaven. What is the other?

- The debate is opened by a brief introduction from Satan.
- It continues with speeches by four of the fallen angels, Moloch, Belial, Mammon and Beëlzebub.
- There is then a vote by the fallen angels.
- Beëlzebub congratulates the assembly on their decision to seek the ruin of Eden and poses the question of who will put the plan into action.
- Satan then volunteers to take on this quest.
- The fallen angels worship and praise Satan.

Satan sits exalted in Pandemonium as the fallen angels, having been cast into the unknown territory of Hell, try to decide what to do next. Moloch advocates the renewal of war, an argument rebutted by Belial point by point. Mammon is concerned that the fallen angels should try to make the best of their situation in Hell. When Beëlzebub speaks, it is clear that he offers a point of view already discussed with Satan, and the vote of the rebels favours the ruining of mankind as the best way forward. Beëlzebub praises this decision and asks who will undertake this task. Satan quickly volunteers and after more than four hundred lines of debate, he has his first substantial speech in Book II (430–66).

COMMENTARY

At the beginning of this Book, Milton in a very succinct (and damning) description presents Satan as a king, with 'barbaric' (4) trappings. Satan's introduction to the debate characterises God as 'the Thunderer' (28). This is one example of a range of negative terms used by the fallen angels to describe God throughout their discussion. The same practice is also adopted by Eve later in *Paradise Lost*, immediately after her fall (Book IX: 815).

In a brilliant piece of **rhetoric**, Satan attempts to suggest in line 23 that his rule in Hell is superior to that of God in Heaven: he argues that because Hell is so terrible, nobody will harbour the ambition of trying to remove Satan from his throne. Satan's eminence, he suggests, serves merely to make him the first target of God's wrath.

When the debate itself gets underway, the focus seems to move away from Satan for the first time in the epic, as the fallen angels debate in Pandemonium. But we are to learn that the whole drift of the discussion has been pre-determined by Satan (378–85). Thus this 'debate' is a parody of later arguments over freewill and pre-destination (see, for example lines 558-61), in that Satan is contriving a situation in which the fallen angels apparently make a choice, but, in reality, he has plotted the outcome in advance.

Milton provides introductory descriptions of each of the speakers, which precede their contributions. These serve to affect our expectations about each speaker's position in the debate. The introduction to Moloch, 'the strongest and the fiercest' (44), leads us to expect that he will argue for war. Belial's introduction, which emphasises his skilful tongue, suggests that he will be more subtle in his argument. Mammon (who, like Beëlzebub, we have met before) is given no introduction, because he needs none: since he represents the love of riches, it is inevitable that he will argue that the fallen angels should seek to discover all the riches and resources of Hell.

The principal speeches in the debate are characterised by their expression of uncertainty. For example, Moloch and Belial ask respectively:

> **CONTEXT**
>
> In Milton's time political debates had been held in Parliament before the Civil War, among the army during the war and in Parliament again during the rule of Cromwell (see **Background: Historical background**). Milton and his readers would, therefore, have had ample experience of the ways in which arguments and proposals were made.

> what can be worse
> Than to dwell here (85–6)

and

> who knows,
> . . . whether our angry Foe
> Can give it, or will ever? (151–3)

The fallen angels do not know what they are capable of, nor of what God is capable. They are also uncertain in the sense that three of the four proposers (Moloch, Belial and Mammon) are prevented by Satan and Beëlzebub from taking part in a real debate.

Moloch expresses uncertainty about what the future might hold, wondering whether the fallen angels can be destroyed, and whether anything can be imagined that is worse than Hell. Belial seizes upon Moloch's uncertainty over what God might do next, and comes to a different conclusion. Belial's eloquence equips him to paint a vivid portrait of how awful the future could be:

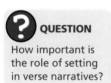

QUESTION

How important is the role of setting in verse narratives?

> what if . . .
> this firmament
> Of Hell should spout her cataracts of fire (174–6)

Belial's principal distinction is the skilfulness of his speech. He can, for example, use irony to emphasise his point (see lines 156–9, where he suggests that God might destroy the fallen angels accidentally or because God has not thought through the consequences). At the same time, he can also offer seemingly rational and comforting suggestions: for example at line 216 he argues that the strength of the fallen angels will allow them to survive their current punishment, and that they may become accustomed ('inured') to it, and that God may eventually ease their plight.

Mammon considers the possibility of God pardoning the fallen angels, and describes this in negative terms of 'Forced hallelujahs' (243) and 'servile offerings' (246) given to an 'envied sovereign' (244). At no point does he, or any of the other fallen angels, consider that they may freely repent, accept God's superiority and worship God of their own volition, without compulsion.

Beëlzebub, seeing that the fallen angels are persuaded by Mammon and are likely to opt for peace, intervenes to suggest the strategy of corrupting humanity in Eden. He again uses negative terms to describe God, such as 'the conqueror' (338), and uses 'God' only in connection with Adam and Eve (368).

In accepting the task to corrupt mankind, Satan begins by emphasising how difficult this expedition will be – so difficult, that it is not surprising that there have been no volunteers. The reader needs to bear in mind that Satan's description of what lies outside Hell is based purely on conjecture: nothing prepares him, or the reader, for what is to be encountered in the later parts of Book II.

As the debate comes to an end (496–505), Milton, in the voice of the **narrator**, laments that even devils keep agreement ('concord') with one another: only the human race shows disagreement, and hypocrisy. This seems to be a comment on the disputes, both military and spiritual, of Milton's own day.

 CHECK THE NET

Among the most celebrated debates during the Civil War were the discussions which took place within the Army in October and November of 1647. These were held in London and are known as the Putney Debates. Detailed discussion of these debates and the background to them can be found at **http://www. putneydebates. com**

GLOSSARY

2	**Ormus** a trading city, famous for its jewels
	Ind India
3	**gorgeous** showy
4	**barbaric pearl and gold** pearl and gold fashioned in an uncivilised country
6	**bad eminence** supremacy in evil
8	**insatiate** with an appetite not to be appeased
9	**success** the outcome of his previous experience
11	**Powers and dominions** these, like 'virtues' in line 15, are ranks of angels (see **Themes: Leadership and authority**)
16	**More glorious and more dread than from no fall** Satan argues that the fall will prove beneficial, in that the fallen angels will be more glorious than they were before. See the commentary above on Book I: 27–298
18	**just right, and the fixed laws** Satan argues that his leadership is somehow legitimate. He has argued in Book I: 639–40 that God's leadership is merely a matter of custom

continued

29	**bulwark** defence
39	**prosperity** the state of having remained in Heaven
42	**We now debate** Satan has been careful to establish the basis for his own leadership in these opening remarks, before he even considers what future action should be taken
50	**recked** cared (as in 'reckless')
51	**sentence** opinion
59	**tyranny** God has now become a tyrant in Moloch's view; in line 64 he uses the word 'Torturer'
64	**meet** match, equal
65	**engine** a machine used in war, such as a battering ram or catapult (see, for example, line 923)
69	**Tartárean** Hellish (from Tartarus, a place of punishment in the underworld of Greek mythology)
70	**torments** Milton probably intended the specific sense of machines used to hurl stones in addition to the general meaning of 'pains'
74	**that forgetful lake** the 'oblivious pool' of Book I: 266
82	**event** outcome
83	**Our Stronger** God
87	**to utter woe** meaning both 'to complete misery' and 'to tell of our misery'
90	**vassals** slaves
99	**if our substance be indeed divine** Moloch cannot know whether or not angels can die
106	**denounced** denoted
113	**manna** the food provided by God for the Israelites in the desert
114	**dash** confound
117	**Timorous** fearful
119	**peers** both 'equals' and 'lords'
124	**he who most excels in fact of arms** Moloch
132	**óbscure** hidden
139	**ethereal mould** the substance of Heaven
150	**the wide womb of uncreated night** Belial describes the area not yet used for creation as 'night' and as a mother ('womb').

CHECK THE BOOK

The term 'womb' is further developed later in Book II, in the story of Sin (778 and 798) and the description of Chaos (911). Satan addresses the rulers of Chaos as 'spirits of this nethermost abyss, / Chaos and ancient Night' (969–70). There are also references to night in Book I: 204 and 503, and in Book II: 439 and 894.

156	**Belike** probably
165	**amain** in haste
166	**besought** looked for
173	**intermitted vengeance** vengeance which has been interrupted
175	**stores** storehouses, resources
	firmament foundation (usually used of Heaven)
176	**cataracts** flood-gates or deluges
177	**Impendent** about to happen
182	**racking** torturing
183	**yon** yonder, over there
188	**dissuades** argues against
189	**him** God
223–5	**since … woe** the sense of these lines can be paraphrased as follows: 'our present situation is a poor form of happiness, but not the worst, provided we do not bring further unhappiness upon ourselves'
245	**ambrosial** Heavenly
250	**leave obtained** permission given (by God)
263–70	**How oft … please?** Mammon here compares the state of the fallen angels with that of God hidden in clouds. He argues that God is still as glorious when hidden, and so the fallen angels can create their own glory in the darkness of Hell
271	**Wants not** is not lacking in
	lustre splendour
275	**our elements** part of our being
278	**sensible** sense, feeling, perception
281	**Compose** come to terms with
285–90	**The assembly … tempest** an **epic simile** comparing the murmuring of the fallen angels to the sound of wind in rocks at sea
287	**cadence** sound (usually signalling the end of a piece of music)
288	**o'erwatched** weary through keeping watch
	bark ship
292	**field** battle

continued

CONTEXT

The word 'motions' (191) is used here in the sense of formal proposals made in a debate, as well as in the more general sense of activities (especially military activities).

294	Michaël the archangel leading the rout of the fallen angels
296	nether underworld
297	policy cunning statesmanship
306	Atlantéan the adjective referring to Atlas who, in Greek mythology, was forced by Jupiter to carry the world on his shoulders
310	Thrones and imperial powers, offspring of Heaven Beëlzebub's opening words echo those of Satan at line 11
312	style manner of address
313	popular vote vote of the people
322	curb restraint
334	stripes from being whipped
336	to our power to the fullest extent we can
348	some new race called Man in Book I: 650–4 we were told the rumour of the creation of Eden and the human race
355	mould type
357	attempted tested
362	their defence the defence of Adam and Eve
367	puny newly created
374	Hurled headlong compare Book I: 45
375	original origins
376	Advise consider
382	confound ruin
384	involve mix
386	augment increase: the **narrator** hints that all will turn out well
	Synod usually a meeting of clergy
402	balm cure, power of healing
406	palpable obscure darkness which can be felt
407	uncouth unknown
409	abrupt abyss
412	senteries sentries: the word needs to have three syllables in order to fit the rhythm of the ten-syllable line. This spelling, along with 'century', was not uncommon in Milton's time

CONTEXT

The phrase 'iron sceptre' (327) is used to signify total control. Beëlzebub's line of argument is that, even in Hell, the fallen angels will remain under the jurisdiction of God. The matter of whether or not the fallen angels control Hell through their occupation of it is one which recurs throughout these opening Books.

415	suffrage selection through a vote
423	Astonished struck with fear
428	monarchal pride the pride of a king; Milton thus compares earthly monarchs with the hellish Satan
430	progeny race or family
435	Outrageous cruel and excessive
	immures encloses
436	adamant an indestructible material
437	egress exit
439	unessential night formless darkness
441	abortive gulf a gulf which threatens to undo the very creation of the traveller
442	scape escape
448	public moment importance to the people
452	Refusing if I refuse
457	intend ponder
462	intermit leave out
470	erst formerly
478	awful full of respect
481	general safety the safety of the majority
484	specious unfounded
490	louring glowering
497	men only only humankind
504	enow enough
508	Midst in the centre
	paramount chief angel
509	antagonist enemy
512	globe throng
513	emblazonry trappings of heraldry
	horrent a variant of 'horrid', meaning 'bristling'
517	sounding alchemy noisy brass
520	returned them answered

CONTEXT

At line 483, with the phrase 'lest bad men should boast', Milton follows the conventional Christian belief that good deeds achieved by men are not won by their own credit but only through the grace of God.

LINES 521–628 – THE DESCRIPTION OF THE FALLEN ANGELS AFTER SATAN'S DEPARTURE

- The fallen angels are described as having six distinct occupations: they race, they ride, they stir up whirlwinds, they sing of their own 'heroic' deeds, they debate philosophy and they explore their new surroundings.

- The description of the last group leads the narrator to a description of the geography of Hell, its four streams and the river Lethe.

CONTEXT

The 'four infernal rivers' mentioned at line 575 are the four rivers or streams of Hades, the Greek underworld. In his description of Hell, Milton draws on the geography and the characteristics of the Ancient Greeks' vision of Hell. Lethe, the river of oblivion or forgetfulness is, in mythological terms, a more significant river than the other four, and merits a more substantial description (see lines 583–6).

Milton describes the ways in which the fallen angels behave after Satan's departure. The overall sense is that all their activity is futile and pointless: they can do no more than 'entertain / The irksome hours' (526–7) until their leader returns. Different levels of detail are given to the description of these activities: the first three are described in a total of eighteen lines; the singing in celebration of the war in Heaven takes up nine lines; the philosophical debate on foreknowledge and freewill is given thirteen lines, whilst the exploration of Hell leads seamlessly into the description of the rivers of Hell.

COMMENTARY

Milton once again displays the breadth and vividness of his imagination. Having described Hell, Satan and the fallen angels, Milton now considers how the rebels could pass their time. The change from the debate to a descriptive section is marked by the inclusion of an **epic simile** (533–5), although the activity which is introduced here is far from heroic, and merely a way for the fallen angels to divert themselves. This has not been an issue in Heaven where the passage of time is not marked as it is in the fallen world. A second epic simile follows almost immediately (542–6) again undercut by being merely an introduction to the fallen angels throwing rocks in their boredom.

Milton gives particular emphasis to the song of the fallen angels (547–50), which takes the form of an epic poem which celebrates their own heroism: Milton is suggesting that previous epics, which have celebrated military heroism, are inferior in subject to his (see **Literary background: The epic tradition**).

The description of the philosophical debate held by the fallen angels (558–61) includes the very areas which have most perplexed readers of *Paradise Lost*, especially the relationship between God's foreknowledge and the free will of humanity. For more on this discussion see **Critical history: Critics on predestination**.

GLOSSARY

522	rangèd drawn up in military order
524	sad choice choice causing only sorrow
526	Truce respite
	entertain while away
528	Part some of them (used likewise at line 531)
	sublime lifted up
530	Pythian games that were held in the ancient Greek city of Delphi every four years
531	shun the goal in the game which they are playing, some of the competitors come close to the pole but fail to hit it
532	fronted face to face, opposing
536	Prick forth advance on horse
	airy belonging to Heaven
	couch lower
538	welkin sky
539	Typhœan giant. This adjective refers back to Typhon, who was mentioned in Book I (196 ff.): in Greek mythology, he and his brother Briareos fought against the god Jupiter. The adjective is therefore very appropriate for the rage of the fallen angels
	fell horrible (with a possible pun on 'fell' the past tense of 'fall')
542–6	As when … sea the basis of this **simile** is an episode from the story of Hercules (Alcides)

continued

CONTEXT

The incident referred to at lines 542–6 is from Greek mythology, where Hercules, returning from battle in Oechalia, sends for a robe to wear when making an offering of thanks to the god Zeus. His wife dips the robe in a love-potion, but its effects prove poisonous to Hercules and cause him to throw the messenger, Lichas, into the sea. The story is related in Ovid's *Metamorphoses*.

543	envenomed drenched in poison
547	Retreated in seclusion
550–1	fate ... force ... chance these terms are employed by the fallen angels throughout the opening Books as ways of accounting for their defeat: they cannot accept the simpler explanation that they were wrong to rebel
552	partial meaning 'biased', 'incomplete' and 'sung in different parts'
554	took with ravishment enchanted
564	apathy calm acceptance
568	obdurèd hardened
570	gross bands large troops
572	clime climate
592	Serbonian bog according to tradition, Lake Serbonis, in Egypt, was bounded by quicksand which had swallowed armies
594	parching drying
595	frore frozen; 'Burns frore' is an oxymoron
596	harpy-footed Furies Milton combines mythological creatures here. Virgil's *Aeneid* has claw-handed Harpies, and Homer's *Odyssey* includes Furies
597	revolutions periods of time
601	pine suffer pain
604	sound stretch of water
611	Medusa one of the three Gorgons, whose hair consisted of serpents. The Gorgons were three sisters in Greek mythology whose eyes turned to stone anyone who looked at them
613	wight creature
614	Tantalus a king in Greek mythology who was punished by being placed in a lake of water which receded whenever he tried to drink
619	dolorous painful
627	fables yet have feigned Milton argues that previous **epics** have dealt with untrue ('feigned') fables; his material, by contrast, is true
628	Hydras and Chimeras monsters of Greek mythology

CONTEXT

Line 600 is one of the last occasions when the word 'starve' is used in this more general sense of 'to perish', and not to mean specifically death through lack of food. This early meaning is, however, still preserved in some dialects of northern England.

LINES 629–1055 – SATAN'S VOYAGE AND HIS ENCOUNTERS WITH SIN, DEATH AND CHAOS

- Satan arrives at the utmost bounds of Hell.
- He meets two monstrous creatures, identified as Sin and Death.
- He then moves on to meet the figure of Chaos and to come within sight of Earth.

Satan moves out of Hell for the first time in the poem and encounters Sin and Death. Death challenges Satan and they are about to fight each other when Sin intervenes and reveals that all three are inter-related. Satan persuades Sin to open the gates of Hell, and he journeys on towards Eden, buffeted by the winds. He comes to the realm of Chaos, a figure whom Satan also wins to his side. Milton emphasises that, although Satan's journey from Hell is arduous, an easy route will be constructed after the fall of mankind from Hell to 'this frail world' (1030) so that Sin and Death may come to visit mankind. At the end of the Book, Satan gets his first glimpse of the universe: 'this pendent world' (1052).

COMMENTARY

Milton introduces us in this section to two formidable shapes, as yet unnamed. We are to learn in line 760 that one is Sin, and, in line 787, that the other is Death. Both are the children of Satan and Milton implicitly evokes a formula that Satan (or Temptation) plus Sin equals Death. This is an echo of the biblical saying 'The wages of sin is Death' (Romans 6:23). That saying also forms the underlying message of Chaucer's *Pardoner's Tale*, to which reference is made elsewhere in these Notes (see **Literary background: The Gothic tradition**). A further biblical source for this saying occurs in James 1:15, where temptation is said to lead to evil actions that in turn lead to death.

We have been told (at the beginning of Book I) that the poem would describe how death and woe came into the world; but we have not been led to expect that these would be represented through allegorical **personifications**.

CONTEXT

Homer's epic poem the *Odyssey* recounts Odysseus's adventures and his return home ten years after the fall of Troy. It may be that the reference to the separation of Sin and Satan is intended to remind the reader of the separation of Penelope and her husband Odysseus: Odysseus went to fight an earthly war, whilst Satan went to fight a war in Heaven.

Milton's technique here owes much to that of the poet Edmund Spenser (?1552–99), whose unfinished work *The Faerie Queene* was the first **epic** poem in English (see **Literary background: The epic tradition**). Spenser's description of Error in Book I of his poem is, like Milton's Sin, half woman and half monster, and she is also pestered by a monstrous brood. A more significant connection, however, is that Spenser very frequently introduces figures to his poem which remain unnamed for many lines, just as Milton does here.

There are two further features of this section which are worthy of comment. One is that Satan's **rhetoric** is demonstrated to be as effective outside Hell as it was within Hell: he is able to use his powers of persuasion to win over Sin and Chaos to be his allies. For example, he tells Sin that:

> I haste
> . . . and . . . shall soon return,
> And bring ye to the place where thou and Death
> Shall dwell at ease (838–41)

The other is that Milton uses a technique here which he is to deploy throughout the epic, and that is to have an incident related by one character to another. Here, Sin relates to Satan the story of her creation and that of Death; later in the poem, Raphael will tell Adam the story of the war in Heaven, and Adam will, in turn, tell Raphael what he knows of his own creation and that of Eve. The reader is thus forced to consider whether these narratives are accurate and truthful, and how they impact on those who hear them. One distinctive feature of the narrative which Sin gives here of her own birth is that the hearer of the narrative, Satan, was actually involved in the event, yet seems to know nothing of it: 'Hast thou forgotten me then,' she asks (747). This is the first of several instances where one character tells another of events which have already taken place (see the **Synopsis** of Books V, VI and VII earlier in this section). (For more about Sin and Milton's description of her, see **Extended commentaries – Text 3**).

At line 835, Satan locates Earth as a place 'more removed', that is 'further away'. Satan's logic leads him to conjecture that humanity

CONTEXT

In Milton's time, the shipping trade was flourishing with Bengal (Bengala) and with the Spice Islands such as Ternate and Tidore (now part of Indonesia). There may be an implication here that, just as the merchants brought 'spicy drugs' (640) to trade, so Satan is about to trade Eve's innocence for the forbidden fruit.

has been situated in a new place, rather than in Heaven, in case the population should increase and rebel. At the very close of the Book, Satan sees the entire universe, described as 'pendent' (1052) or hanging. The narrative itself becomes pendent at this point, as the focus moves, in Books III and IV, to Heaven.

> **? QUESTION**
>
> Are the final lines of the last Book of the epic a closure, or do they also make the readers look forwards?

GLOSSARY

633	scours moves quickly through
636–43	As when ... fiend another **epic simile**, based upon sea voyages
636	descried caught sight of
637	equinoctial equally by day and night
642	Ply stemming make headway against the wind
645	thrice threefold see line 436
648	unconsumed see Book I: 69
655	Cerbérean Cerberus was the monstrous many-headed dog guarding the entrance to Hell in classical mythology
656	list wished
658	kennel live (like dogs in a kennel)
660	Scylla one of two mythological monsters (the other being Charybdis) guarding the straits of Messina
662	night-hag Hecate, queen of witchcraft in Greek mythology
672	dart spear
673	kingly crown just as Satan had exhibited 'monarchal pride' (428), so here Death wears a kingly crown. Milton contrives to make every reference of kingship evil
677	The undaunted fiend Satan
678	Admired wondered
683	athwart across
686	Retire move back
687	Hell-born, not to contend with spirits of Heaven Satan claims superiority over Death, whom he assumes to be a creature of Hell rather than a fallen angel, like himself
693	Conjured joined together
696	reckon'st compares. Death challenges the claim that Satan is a spirit of Heaven
702	lingering delaying

continued

CONTEXT

The revelation that Death is Satan's 'only son' (line 728) comes as a surprise to the reader and to Satan. Sin also identifies herself as Satan's daughter. Their relationship is, in part, a **parody** of that between God and the Son, partly a parody of Eve's creation from Adam's side, and partly an **allusion** to the Greek myth of the birth of Athena.

CONTEXT

Athena was the Greek goddess of wisdom, war, the arts, industry, justice and skill. She was the favourite child of Zeus, and sprang fully grown out of her father's head, already dressed in armour. Thus, Sin, Adam and Athena are created without being born of woman.

709	**Ophiucus** a constellation
710	**hair** the Greek word for comet (708) literally means 'hairy star'
	snaky sorceress Sin
735	**Hellish pest** Death ('pest' was a more forceful term in Milton's time than it is now)
736	**Forbore** ceased
738	**sudden** impetuous
739	**Prevented** forestalled
741	**double-formed** i.e. half woman, half serpent
	Portentous exciting admiration
768	**fields** wars
771	**empyrean** Heavens
772	**pitch** height
780	**Prodigious** both enormous and monstrous
785	**inbred enemy** i.e. Death – 'inbred' because literally bred (born) inside Sin
798	**list** wish
800	**repast** food
801	**vex** cause pain (stronger than the modern use of the word)
803	**in opposition** facing one another
808	**bane** poison
814	**he who reigns above** God
815	**lore** lesson
818	**my fair son** a supreme piece of Satanic irony: the ugly Death is anything but 'fair'
819	**dalliance** sexual pleasure
827	**uncouth errand** mission of which the outcome is unknown
829	**unfounded deep** depths as yet unmeasured
831	**concurring** to the same effect
	ere before
832	**round** thoroughly and perfectly formed
833	**purlieus** outskirts
834	**supply** fill up
835	**vacant room** the space left behind by our absence

837	broils disputes
842	buxom unresisting
847	maw stomach
859	office employment, service
864	author origin. Eve uses this same word in addressing Adam in Book IV: 635
869	voluptuous giving pleasure
877	wards parts of a lock
883	Érèbus Hell
900	embryon undeveloped
904	Barca … Cyréné cities in north Africa
910	Chance having hitherto been referred to in abstract, Chance is now **personified**, as are Rumour, Tumult, Confusion and Discord (965–7)
919	frith firth, a narrow inlet of the sea
922	Bellona the name of the goddess of war in Roman mythology, here used to represent war itself
927	vans front wings
933	pennons wings
935	chance see note to lines 550–1
937	nitre saltpetre, one of the ingredients of gunpowder
939	Syrtis sandbank
943	gryphon a legendary creature who guarded gold, which the Arimaspians (one-eyed monsters) attempted to steal (945)
962	sable-vested black-clothed
964	Orcus and Adès two names for the god of Hell
965	Demogorgon another classical god of Hell
980	profound depth
982	behoof advantage
988	the anarch old Chaos
992	Made head revolted
1012	alacrity liveliness
1016	Environed encircled
1017	Argo the ship sailed by the classical hero Jason
1018	Bosphorus the straits of Constantinople

continued

CONTEXT

Sin recalls her sexual relationship with Satan: 'such joy thou took'st / With me in secret' (765–6). If Satan is the father of Sin (727), there must be a question as to whether their sexual liaison constitutes incest. This matter is not raised in the case of Adam and Eve, because he is never referred to as her father. What is very clear is that the sexual relationship between Sin and Death is both incestuous and a rape (792–4).

CHECK THE BOOK

The phrase 'His dark materials' (916) is the overall title for a trilogy of novels by Philip Pullman. Pullman's work is a fascinating commentary on *Paradise Lost*, and one which is implicitly critical of the beliefs which underpin Milton's epic, especially the seeking after forbidden knowledge. Pullman applauds this endeavour, whilst Milton condemns it.

1019	Ulysses the Roman name for Odysseus, one of the principal classical heroes. He is the central character in Homer's epic *Odyssey*
	larboard left side
1024	amain at full speed
1030	this frail world Earth
1042	Wafts sails
	dubious wavering
1055	Accursed ... a cursèd a pun: Satan is damned ('Accursed') and the time when he encounters Eden is the hour of damnation ('a cursed hour')
	hies hastens

EXTENDED COMMENTARIES

TEXT 1 – BOOK I LINES 44–83

From 'Him the Almighty Power' to 'thus began'

This passage comes shortly after the very beginning of the poem. It introduces us to the power of God and to the nature of Hell.

The process of naming is highlighted in this extract. There are three principal participants in this passage, all of whom are named: God, Satan and Beëlzebub, although the company of fallen angels is also mentioned, referred to as 'his horrid crew' (51) and 'the companions of his fall' (76). We learn from lines 80–2 that, while Satan has already received his name, Beëlzebub will acquire his name much later in Palestine: Milton attempts to make his poem encompass the whole of history. The power of God, and of God's control, is immediately emphasised. It is that power which dominates the entire epic.

Almost all of the epic, and certainly all of its first two Books, takes place before time began, yet the poet needs to find a mechanism for describing the passage of time. He does so here, for example, by referring to the time it took for the fall to take place as 'Nine times the space that measures day and night / To mortal men' (50–1). By including reference to 'mortal men' (51) and by referring to human history in the naming of Beëlzebub, Milton makes us part of the action of his poem.

The poem operates by moving between Heaven, Hell and Eden and by emphasising the differences between these three distinct regions. This section is dominated by the description of the pain of Hell, contrasted with two brief references to Heaven, as 'the ethereal sky' (45) and as 'the place from whence they fell' (75). The poem also consistently deals in extremes and superlatives: everything about the regions which it describes is incomparable. Throughout, Milton uses terms such as 'bottomless', 'omnipotent', 'ever-burning', 'unconsumed', 'utter' and 'utmost'.

The passage demonstrates the care which readers must employ in coming to *Paradise Lost*. On the one hand, the overall meaning of the passage should be clear enough, even on the first reading; on the other hand, more careful examination will reveal the great subtlety of Milton's writing. For example, a modern-day reader may be surprised by the use of 'utter' as a term expressing extremes. In Milton's time 'utter' meant 'outer', just as 'utmost' signified 'outermost'. Similarly, the term 'horrid' is not nowadays a particularly powerful word, but in Milton's day it could carry the sense of 'terrifying' or 'revolting'.

Milton is famous – perhaps even notorious – for the scope of his **allusions**, both biblical and classical. Some readers will find this reputation daunting, but this extract demonstrates very clearly that we do not have to possess Milton's breadth of knowledge to appreciate *Paradise Lost*. There are at least two classical allusions in this passage: one, in the nine days of the fall, to the fall of the Titans in Hesiod's ancient Greek *Theogony*; the other, in the reference to the absence of hope, to Dante's fourteenth-century *Inferno*. However, readers who do not immediately recognise these allusions are not prevented from understanding the meaning of the passage.

One of the most notable features of this extract is a classic instance of the literary figure called the **oxymoron**: 'yet from those flames /

CONTEXT

William Golding was sufficiently struck by the **oxymoron** 'Darkness visible' to use it as the title for his 1979 novel; twenty-five years earlier he had taken the translation of 'Beëlzebub' (which derives from Hebrew) as the title for his first novel, *Lord of the Flies*. It is a sign of the influence which Milton has exercised that several later writers have taken their titles from *Paradise Lost*, including Philip Pullman with *His Dark Materials* and John Steinbeck with his novel *In Dubious Battle*.

No light, but rather darkness visible' (62–3). 'Darkness visible' is a **paradox**: darkness cannot be seen. Yet Milton's use of this paradox is a powerful and graphic description of the extent of the darkness in Hell, so terrible and palpable as to seem visible.

The whole of *Paradise Lost* is written in **blank verse**. When blank verse is used at its most straightforward, each line takes the form of a single sentence. At the very beginning of this extract, however, far from having each sentence bound by a single line, Milton begins a new sentence in the middle of a line and runs it on into the next. Moreover, in order to add a greater sense of cohesion between the different parts of the sentence, he includes **alliteration**, which he continues across three lines: 'Him', 'Hurled', 'headlong' and 'hideous' (44–6). As a further example of this play between **syntax** and **metre**, Milton seems almost to be ready to bring the sentence to a close towards the end of line 46, only to use the final syllable of the line to begin a new phrase: 'down / To bottomless perdition' (46–7). Just as the sense of the passage is of an endless process of fall, so this bold use of the metre reinforces that motion being perpetually renewed.

CONTEXT

As an indication of the care with which Milton writes (and, therefore, the care which the reader must exercise), it should be noted that Beëlzebub echoes these words as he anticipates the fall of man in Book II: 373–5: 'his darling sons / Hurled headlong to partake with us, shall curse / Their frail original, and faded bliss.'

There is a particular kind of thematic contrast in the middle of this extract, where Milton places 'peace' and 'rest' (65–6) on the one hand and 'torture without end' (67) on the other. This is a significant distinction, not least because much of literature is concerned with the glorification of movement and ambition, giving little credit to peace and stillness. *Paradise Lost*, however, seeks to emphasise the negative aspects of change, especially the folly of seeking to change what is perfect. The urging of endless torture in this extract is mirrored by the reaction of Satan to Eve and Adam in Book IV: 509–11. There, he recognises that what they experience is love, while his fate is to have:

> neither joy nor love, but fierce desire,
> Among our other torments not the least,
> Still unfulfilled, with pain of longing pines

The dominant **metaphor** of this extract is that of the sea voyage. Satan and his companions, his 'crew', have been 'rolling in the fiery gulf' (51–2), and are now 'o'erwhelmed / With floods and whirlwinds' (76–7); Beëlzebub himself is 'weltering' (78) (one of Milton's favourite words). The subtlety of this metaphor has not always been fully appreciated, because we tend to think of Hell simply as a lower region. This metaphor of the voyage emphasises not only the pain of the process of the fall, but also the idea that the fallen angels are condemned never to find a stable landing place. Even in Hell they continue to be overwhelmed and to welter.

TEXT 2 – BOOK II LINES 430–73

From 'O progeny' to 'must earn'

This extract largely takes the form of a speech by Satan. It is a relatively straightforward passage, which foretells his plans to journey from Hell, and is certainly no more difficult to comprehend than many speeches from plays by Shakespeare. (For further discussion of the perceived difficulty of Milton's language, see **Critical approaches: Language and style.**)

This is a stirring piece of **rhetoric**, and the flaws of Satan's argument are apparent only after careful re-reading and reflection. On first acquaintance, the reader is likely to be impressed by his speech, and it is only after the voice of the **narrator** intervenes at line 466, to reveal Satan's anxiety about others volunteering, that we are sent back to revise our initial views. Milton is extremely skilful in luring his readers into finding Satan admirable: a comparable instance occurs in Book I: 615–21 where Satan is moved to tears by the sight of his fellow rebels.

The passage is very revealing of the character of Satan, and of the tactics he employs to maintain control over his fallen troops. The speech begins by emphasising the difficulty of the task of tempting mankind, detailing the terrors of leaving Hell:

> Our prison strong, this huge convéx of fire,
> Outrageous to devour, immures us round
> Ninefold (434–6)

The prospective journey which Satan describes draws upon the dangers of seafaring in Milton's time: the references to 'gulf' (441)

QUESTION

In the passage that immediately follows this extract, Milton describes the ways in which the fallen angels entertain themselves as they wait for the return of Satan. Since this passage doesn't advance the plot of the poem at all, why do you think Milton included it?

and 'coasts' (464) would have had specifically nautical connotations for Milton's contemporary readers.

Yet this presention of danger by Satan is spurious, for he is actually volunteering to mount an escape, and we learn from the final lines of the passage, after the speech has ended, that Satan is anxious to ensure that he alone is able to embark upon this journey, not least because he wants to have all the glory that might accrue from this enterprise.

Another tactic which Satan employs is to flatter his troops. They are not, as far as he is concerned, fallen angels, but rather 'progeny of Heaven' (430): he even uses the formal title 'thrones', which is the name of one of the orders of angels: these names are largely derived from the ways in which angels are described in the Bible (see **Themes: Leadership and authority**).

 QUESTION

Why do you think that the struggle between Satan and God, as portrayed in *Paradise Lost*, continues to have such an appeal for critics of the poem?

Flattery is a device Satan employs later in Book II when he encounters Death (687). If the fallen angels are 'peers' (in the sense of both 'equals' and 'lords'), then Satan's leadership of them makes him all the more exalted.

As he comes to the end of the speech, Satan sets his fellow rebels two tasks: they are to make Hell as tolerable as possible, and to guard against 'a wakeful foe' (463). Yet there is no real indication that the fallen angels know how to accomplish the first task: in the passage that follows they are shown to occupy themselves with trivial pursuits. As for the second task, its very imposition demonstrates how little understanding Satan has of God: he still believes that God intends to visit Hell and impose further torment on the fallen angels. Even if this were the case, there is no basis for Satan to believe that God could be repulsed, however watchful the rebel angels might be.

TEXT 3 – BOOK II LINES 746–814

From 'To whom' to 'none can resist'

In this passage, Sin recounts her own story to Satan, part of which she has experienced with him, and part of which he is unaware.

Sin is a fallen being, like Satan, who, like him, was once fair. In her account, she was created from Satan at the very moment when he conceived of the notion of rebellion against God. Thus, one immediate consequence of the fall of the angels is the birth of Sin.

It may seem strange that Satan does not recognise Sin or recall such a dramatic event as her creation, but this is in part because her appearance has changed, grossly distorted by the birth of her child, but also because this is one of a pattern of **allusions** to forgetfulness which occur throughout these opening two Books. Satan describes his fellow rebels in the first Book as lying 'astonished on the oblivious pool' (266), where 'oblivious' means a state of unconsciousness or unawareness; slightly later (301) these same legions are described as 'entranced'; finally, in Book II, we find an extensive description of the geography of Hell which includes (583 ff.) the river Lethe, the river of forgetfulness.

Sin tells how she sprang fully grown from Satan's left side in a **parodic** foreshadowing of the creation of Eve from Adam's side in Book VII. The immediate reaction of the rebel angels was to be repulsed by her, but she won them over, Satan in particular. Milton, by using a **personification** of Sin as a female figure, is able to make Sin possessed of an alluring sensuality.

However, despite the mutual attraction between Sin and Satan, she is able to view the war in Heaven differently. She sees the victory of God's angels as being inevitable, although she associates herself with the losers:

> to our part loss and rout
> Through all the empyrean (770–1)

Her speech is finely crafted by Milton: it includes balance ('to our almighty Foe . . . to our part' (769–70); **alliteration** 'fields . . . fought' (768); the repetition of 'down' to intensify the idea of the fall (771–2); and, once again, the inclusion of the word 'headlong' (772) used earlier to describe both the fall of the angels and, in anticipation, the fall of man.

QUESTION

Why should Sin be able to speak so persuasively when her appearance is so repulsive? What might this indicate about the relationship between Satan and Sin?

Sin was separated from Satan, and Death was born as her son. That birth was painful to the mother – a presaging of the pain of childbirth which is to be one of the outcomes of the fall of man later in the **epic**. The adjectives used in this part of the extract dwell on pain and suffering: 'rueful throes' (780), 'odious offspring' (781), 'violent way' (782), 'fatal dart' (786). The latter is a particularly appropriate adjective because this child is Death.

Sin is described in a powerfully repellent way in this evocative passage (all the more so since the description comes directly from her): Death was born by being torn from Sin's entrails (783), and he pursues his mother 'Inflamed with lust' (791).

Like the fallen angels, and like the innocent Adam and Eve before their fall, Sin did not know what death might be, and so cried out in pain as she gave birth, only to find that, in doing so, she had given a name to her monstrous child. The relationship between Death and Sin becomes even more perverted than that between Sin and Satan: Sin is the daughter of Satan, yet gave birth to his child; Death is the son of Sin yet raped his mother who gives birth to further children each hour who torment her, gnawing at her very body.

Sin's first child has a name, but the subsequent 'yelling monsters' (795) remain unnamed and indistinguishable one from another. By this stage, the reader should have become attuned to the significance of using names across the whole of these first two Books (for further examples see **Extended commentaries – Text 1**).

We are also accustomed to the presentation of uncertainty on the part of the fallen angels, and Sin shares their lack of knowledge. She knows that Death depends on her to escape his own demise, but she is not clear on exactly how and when this might come to pass:

> knows that I
> Should prove a bitter morsel, and his bane
> Whenever that shall be (807–9)

Milton is careful in his representation of Sin: she is more than simply a **personification**. Milton makes her the child of Satan, and reveals later in Book II that she can have access to mankind only

CONTEXT

Many of the characteristics of Milton's description of Sin are drawn from the monstrous Scylla of Greek mythology (referred to in Book II: 660) who features both in the *Odyssey* (Book XII) and the *Aeneid* (Book II). Milton also draws upon the description of Error in Book I of Spenser's *The Faerie Queene* (Canto 1, Stanza 14).

after Satan has been successful in tempting Eve and Adam. Thus, in Book X, Sin and Death are represented as being constant presences in the lives of humanity, whereas Satan, who is directly responsible for the creation of Sin and Death, leaves Eden (and the Earth) in Book X to return to Hell.

CHECK THE BOOK

Sin and Death reappear in Book X of *Paradise Lost* (lines 230 onwards), and are portrayed first as sitting at the gates of Hell waiting for Satan's return from Eden, and then as fashioning the road which leads from 'this now fenceless world' (302) to Hell.

PART THREE

CRITICAL APPROACHES

CHARACTERISATION

Readers of these Notes will find that these observations on the main characters in the opening Books of *Paradise Lost* can be amplified by being read alongside the **Detailed summaries** and **glossaries** in **Part Two**.

GOD

Milton suggests at the outset of his poem that the theme for his **epic** as a whole is to 'justify the ways of God to men' (Book I: 26). In the first two Books he can accomplish only part of this aim, and, by beginning the action in Hell rather than in Heaven, Milton has made a deliberate choice of focus, one which conditions the way the reader receives and evaluates the presentation of God.

We learn of God in two ways in the opening Books – through what is said about him by Satan and the other characters, and through the comments of the **narrator**. Though God does not appear directly, the reader is constantly aware of God's presence and of his influence on the characters to which we are introduced.

 CHECK THE POEM
Poems in praise of the Creator God can be found from the earliest period of English literature, but the idea of presenting the Creator himself as a character in the narrative probably derives from the Mystery Plays of the Middle Ages (see **Sin, Death and Chaos** below).

Apart from the narrator, all those who speak in the opening two Books see themselves as victims of God's power. Chief among these are Satan and the angels who have rebelled and fallen with him, but, at the end of Book II, we encounter Sin and Death, two further characters whose very existence is a direct result of the rebellion against God.

In these circumstances, we are unlikely to receive unbiased views of God from those who speak about him. Milton, therefore, allows the fallen angels to reveal themselves and their true natures through the ways in which they describe God. For example, Satan's early negative descriptions of God are based on no evidence whatsoever, merely on speculation. He claims in Book I lines 123–4 that God is at that very moment triumphant and joyful over the defeat of the rebel angels, and, a few lines later, that God is 'vengeful' (148). Satan has no basis for these claims, any more than he has for using any negative terms (for example, 'the angry victor', Book I: 169) to describe God or God's motives.

Nevertheless, so skilful is Milton's portrayal of the fallen angels that a grudging acknowledgement of the power of God lurks beneath their words. One early example of this can be found in Book I, where Beëlzebub acknowledges that God must indeed be almighty if he could defeat such a mighty force as that of the rebel angels: 'he our Conqueror, (whom I now / Of force believe almighty, since no less / Than such could have o'erpowered such force as ours)' (144–6).

In some respects, God lies outside the action even in those Books in which he appears. He is the creator of everything within the poem, and readers come to realise that Milton goes to some lengths to present God as unbiased and objective. When Satan rebels, God does not lead the troops of faithful angels himself, nor does he personally visit Adam and Eve to warn them of the approach of Satan. He does not dismiss them from Eden, nor does He become mortal to redeem fallen humanity.

Milton skilfully effects a **parody** of this objective God in the relationship between Satan and Beëlzebub.

SATAN

Satan is, in some respects, the most significant figure in the entire poem. He is the only character to be present in all of its three principal locations (Hell, Heaven and Eden) as well as passing through the region separating Hell and Eden in the second half of Book II.

He is the first figure we meet, and he is presented as the leader of the rebel angels who find themselves in Hell. In particular, Satan seeks to find some point of stability and security in this new and uncertain environment. He looks within himself for the source of this stability, referring to his 'fixed mind' (Book I: 97) and his 'mind not to be changed' (Book I: 253). However, like the other angels who find themselves in Hell after their rebellion, the extent of

CHECK THE POEM
Milton wrote little about his own personal relationship with God. Only in Sonnet XIX (which begins 'When I consider how my life is spent') is there anything like that sense of a dialogue between God and the poet that we find in the works of John Donne and George Herbert (these near-contemporaries of Milton are further discussed in **Part Five** of these Notes).

Satan's real uncertainty of mind is revealed in the first word he speaks. His opening speech begins 'If', and the fallen angels wrestle throughout these opening Books with their lack of knowledge about what the future might bring: again and again they ask 'what if' (for example, Book I: 143).

Satan attempts to use his considerable powers of imagination and oratory to change the environment of Hell, and to make what is clearly monstrous and terrifying appear acceptable and even desirable. Early in the opening Book he declares that 'The mind is its own place, and in itself / Can make a Heaven of Hell, a Hell of Heaven' (254–5). This audacious claim to an ability to use language to alter reality is, in a sense, an extension of Satan's most notable attribute, his powers of **rhetoric** and flattery.

For much of the opening two Books of *Paradise Lost* Satan's speeches are public rather than private. We see him speaking to rally his troops in Book I and participating in formal debate and boasting of his prowess in Book II. Only rarely are we given a glimpse of his real sense of pain, for example:

> the thought
> Both of lost happiness and lasting pain
> Torments him (Book I: 54–6)

Certainly this inner torment is never revealed to his peers. His speeches are thus designed to persuade and to flatter.

His initial approach to the fallen angels begins by reminding them of the titles which they formerly enjoyed: 'Princes, potentates, / Warriors, the flower of Heaven' (Book I: 315–6); and he is still addressing them by these titles in Book II: 'Powers and dominions, deities of Heaven' (11).

He flatters Beëlzebub in a parallel fashion:

> him, who in the happy realms of light,
> Clothed with transcendent brightness, didst outshine
> Myriads (Book I: 85–7)

QUESTION

The opening Books of *Paradise Lost* are full of references to the various orders of angels: in Book V lines 600–1, God invokes the names of the orders of angels, while just a few lines further on (772–3), Satan invokes these titles with a very different emphasis. What effect do you think these references are intended to have?

To Satan it seems that the method most likely to rouse his fallen peers is to remind them of how great they once were. To some extent, the description of Belial at the beginning of Book II: 110–17 replicates some of the qualities of satanic flattery and exposes its falseness.

Perhaps the most ironic instance of Satan's flattery, and the example which best illustrates its hollowness, comes at the end of Book II, in his meeting with Sin and Death. His initial reaction to these hideous monsters is: 'nor ever saw till now / Sight more detestable than him and thee' (744–5). Yet when he has finally realised who these creatures are and what their relationship to him is, his mode of address changes to 'Dear daughter' and 'my fair son' (817 and 818).

Satan exercises a fascination for readers partly because his is the first voice we hear (see **Part Three: Satan and drama**), but also because he seems to have certain characteristics which we readily identify as 'human'. For example, in Book I line 118, Satan speaks of having learned from experience, and of profiting from that experience in future actions. We are very accustomed to this process in our own lives, but we may easily fail to see that Satan's experience and his capacity to learn from it is intimately linked with his fallen state. Satan seems to be like us because he demonstrates aspects of being fallen, as humans do.

Satan remains attractive, despite having fallen from Heaven, and remains able to persuade others to his viewpoint. In these opening two Books we see this ability as he convinces his fellow rebels as well as Sin and Chaos simply through the force of his verbal reasoning. The only character on whom he does not use this skill is Death, where the contest becomes more like the martial encounters of traditional, classical **epics**.

Further discussion of Satan, especially in relation to the source of the character in drama, can be found later in this section, while Satan's remarkable appearance is discussed in **Detailed summaries – Book 1 Lines 27–298**.

CHECK THE POEM
Satan is the most prominent in a long line of Miltonic characters who tempt others: Comus tries to tempt the Lady in *Comus*, whilst the entire action of *Samson Agonistes* consists of tempting offers made by a succession of visitors to Samson. In *Paradise Regained*, his sequel to *Paradise Lost*, Milton considers the temptation of Jesus Christ by Satan.

There is also further description of Satan in Book II lines 629–43, when, as he prepares to leave Hell, he uses his ability to fly, as he did in Book I line 225. It is that ability which allows Satan, the 'flying fiend' (Book II: 643), to bring his temptation to Eve and Adam in Eden.

BEËLZEBUB

Beëlzebub is depicted in the opening Books as Satan's chief supporter and his right-hand man. He is the second of the fallen angels to which we are introduced in Book I, second only in importance to Satan himself, and has a crucial role in the debate at the beginning of Book II. He must appear then to be as neutral as the other speakers in the debate, whilst, at the same time, advancing an argument which the narrator tells us (379–80) has already been rehearsed between Satan and Beëlzebub.

QUESTION

Where else in Books I and II does the **narrator** challenge what the fallen angels say?

There are two matters worthy of note here. Firstly, the narrator does not show us this plotting between Satan and Beëlzebub, and so we are surprised to learn that it has taken place (for more on this see **Narrative form and structure**). Secondly, Satan does not himself speak in this debate: his silence might appear at first as indicating his impartiality, but that is revealed to be an illusion, since, in effect, Beëlzebub speaks for Satan.

In the case of God and Satan, readers can gain only an incomplete picture of their characters from the first two Books of the epic, but that picture is developed later in the poem. Beëlzebub has his role entirely confined to Books I and II. Even Sin, Death and Chaos re-appear later in the poem, Beëlzebub does not. We learn almost nothing about the appearance of Beëlzebub in Book I except that, according to Satan's first speech to him, he used to look 'transcendent' (Book I: 86). In a sense, Beëlzebub represents all of the fallen angels, and therefore has only a glorious past and no hope of a future.

In Book II, as Beëlzebub prepares to speak in the great debate, Milton provides a further physical description of him (and thus allows our impression of Beëlzebub to develop incrementally). He seems to be 'A pillar of state' (302) and is able to bear the 'weight of mightiest monarchies' (307) on his huge 'Atlantean' shoulders (306). These allusions to politics and kingship carry negative connotations for Milton.

SIN, DEATH AND CHAOS

Satan and Beëlzebub are represented by Milton in humanised terms, and it is not inappropriate to use the term 'character' in relation to that representation. However, Sin, Death and Chaos are presented very differently, in that they are representations of abstract qualities: they are **personifications**. This kind of representation has a long history in English literature, especially in drama. For example, in the early sixteenth-century play, *Everyman*, the central character has friends called Fellowship, Kindred, Cousin and Goods, all of whom are presented on stage.

In these dramas, the personifications are very precise in terms of their characterisation, in that they represent a single quality. It is one indication of the maturity of English drama in the late sixteenth century that these single-quality, abstract figures become fully-developed, human characters. A character like the villainous Edmund in Shakespeare's *King Lear* owes much to the abstract personifications of the morality plays, but he is far more complex, far more rounded.

There is no biblical precedent for Sin, Death and Chaos, and they are simple characters: Sin is voluptuous and sensual, Death is angry and rapacious, and Chaos presides over figures of uncertainty such as Night, Rumour, Chance, Tumult, Confusion and Discord. They have a single role to play in Book II, and that is to check Satan's progress and, in the case of Sin and Chaos, be won over by him. For Chaos, what Satan offers is entirely false, but this is an accurate foretaste of the methodology which Satan will employ to lure Eve into tasting the forbidden fruit. For further discussion of Sin and Death, see **Extended commentaries – Text 3**.

 CHECK THE NET
Everyman is a type of play now known as a Morality Play, a dramatic genre which developed in the fifteenth century and was designed to teach moral principles without being directly based upon stories from the Bible, as were the Mystery Plays which preceded it. The Luminarium site – **www.luminarium. org** – has a section on Medieval Plays which includes further information on Morality Plays. The site includes links to several examples of the genre.

THEMES

UNCERTAINTY AND INSTABILITY

Milton exercises his imagination, and that of his readers, by attempting to describe the very beginnings of time and place. As his poem opens, the first ever event, the war in Heaven, has only just taken place, and the characters have simply no idea what might happen next, nor what the qualities might be of the environment in which they now find themselves.

The action of these opening Books takes place within a context of uncertainty, and this is represented in two principal forms. On the one hand, the physical spaces described, Hell and the regions of Chaos and Night through which Satan travels, are of uncertain character, and the fallen angels are represented as being unclear about the limits and nature of these regions. On the other hand, the rebel angels are also unclear about their own nature. They are aware that they are not as they were before their fall, but they are uncertain about the extent and the implications of this change.

The physical environment in these first two Books is frequently described in terms of images of sea and night. For example, in Book I, Satan urges Beëlzebub to seek a 'dreary plain' (180):

> Thither let us tend
> From off the tossing of these fiery waves;
> There rest, if any rest can harbour there. (183–6)

Hell is not simply a place of fire, it is a place which lacks the stability of solid ground, and lacks the security of sunlight. These are appropriate images for uncertainty: even today, we know far less about what is in the sea than about the land, and we feel less safe travelling in the dark than by day. In the seventeenth century the sea must have seemed a very challenging environment indeed. Milton is drawing upon the knowledge his contemporary readership would have had of exploration and voyages, their fascination with travel and perhaps their fear. Satan tries to represent Hell as a new-found place which he and the fallen angels have colonised, rather than recognising that God controls them there just as much as he does elsewhere.

CONTEXT

Among the most notable explorers of Elizabethan times were Sir Francis Drake (who sailed to the continent of North America) and Sir Walter Raleigh (who began the colonisation of Virginia). Others who sailed under the patronage of Queen Elizabeth included Sir Humphrey Gilbert (Raleigh's half-brother), Sir John Hawkins, Sir Richard Grenville and Sir Martin Frobisher.

In one of the first extended images of the poem, that of the
Leviathan or whale (beginning at Book I line 201), Milton describes
Satan in terms of the duplicity and uncertainty of the sea. The
vastness of the Leviathan misleads the sailors, lost at night, into
thinking that they have found the security of an island. In reality,
they have found only a whale.

When Satan prepares to leave Hell, another image from the sea is
employed (Book II: 636 ff.), this time quite explicitly to do with
trade by sea. Satan is characterised as being like a merchant bringing
exotic and unfamiliar cargo from distant lands: he is, in fact,
bringing temptation to Eden.

As *Paradise Lost* continues, the sense of uncertainty goes on: it does
not end with these opening two Books. Just as the fallen angels are
unsure about their own nature, so too are Eve and Adam: when we
first encounter them in Book IV, Adam talks to Eve about the
commandment not to eat of the fruit of the tree of knowledge and
the consequence of disobedience:

> So near grows death to life, what e'er death is,
> Some dreadful thing no doubt; for well thou know'st
> God hath pronounced it death to taste that tree. (425–7)

The difference between the uncertainty of Satan and that of Adam
and Eve is that the uncertainty of Adam and Eve is born from their
innocence: as long as they remain innocent, their uncertainty need
never be a threat. Satan's uncertainty, on the other hand, arises from
his having rebelled and placed himself in a new relationship with
God, the nature of which Satan does not understand.

At the close of Book II, Satan encounters the forces of darkness and
Chaos, and this entire passage is again couched in terms of
metaphors of the sea. The gates which Sin lets open reveal 'The
secrets of the hoary deep – a dark / Illimitable ocean without
bound' (891–2). Satan, having come to terms with this environment,
is described as 'glad that now his sea should find a shore' (1011)
and, as he comes to the edge of Chaos, Satan finds himself 'like a
weather-beaten vessel' which 'holds / Gladly the port, though
shrouds and tackle torn' (1043–4).

 QUESTION

Why should the
sea be regarded as
a suitable way of
describing
uncertainty? What
metaphor would
you use to describe
uncertainty?

PURITANISM AND CHRISTIANITY

The Puritans were a group of English Protestants who formed in opposition to Elizabeth I's reformation of the Church of England. Milton was a fierce advocate on behalf of the Puritan cause. He supported it all his adult life against the established Church (the Church of England), which he, like his fellow Puritans, saw as corrupt and too dependent on ritual, on elaborate church buildings and on authoritarian church leaders – bishops, in particular. The Puritans did not believe in the authority of ordained clergy, but in a priesthood of all believers, in simplicity in worship, and the exclusion of vestments and religious images and icons.

Although the Puritans were united in dislike of, and opposition to, ritualised religion, as represented by Archbishop Laud, they found that having apparently defeated that enemy (Laud was beheaded in 1645), the different denominations within the non-conformist churches had little in common; they knew what they were opposed to, but it was more difficult to define what they shared.

Even the term Puritan itself largely originated as a term of abuse employed by opponents of Puritanism (just as to be described as a 'radical' at this time was by no mean positive). In 1665 Thomas Fuller wrote in his *Church History of Britain*: 'The English Bishops … began … urging the clergy to subscribe to the liturgy, ceremonies, discipline of the Church, and such as refused … were branded with the odious name of Puritans, a name which in this notion first began in this year [1564]' (Volume IX Section 66, cited in *The Oxford English Dictionary* under 'Puritan').

Paradise Lost is, of course, a Christian poem, grounded in Milton's own biblical theology. It is also a Christian poem written by a Puritan. Thus, when Milton describes the gathering of the fallen angels in Book I, he uses an image evoking the attacks by the barbarians on Rome:

> A multitude like which the populous North
> Poured never from her frozen loins to pass

CONTEXT

William Laud (1573–1645) was Archbishop of Canterbury from 1633 to 1645, for the greater part of the reign of Charles I. Laud opposed the attempts of the Puritans to reform the Church. He was also a close adviser to the king in the years that led up to the beginning of the Civil War.

Rhene or the Danaw, when her barbarous sons
Came like a deluge on the South. (351–4)

In essence, Milton is describing here an attack upon Rome, the
foremost city of the Catholic Church, and describing that attack in
negative terms. This might seem odd, given Milton's avowed anti-
Catholicism.

The point is that Milton is not defending Catholicism in this **simile**:
he is defending Christian civilisation: at the time when these
barbarian hordes attacked Rome (AD 455), there was no other form
of Christianity except Catholicism.

Milton's Puritanism comes to the fore in subtle ways in the first
Book of *Paradise Lost*. At the very beginning of the poem, while
invoking his Muse, he addresses the Holy Spirit in these terms:
'And chiefly thou, O Spirit, that dost prefer / Before all temples the
upright heart and pure' (17–18).

Milton asserts that the Holy Spirit, part of the Christian divine
Trinity, disapproves of elaborate and ritualised religious practices,
just as Milton himself disapproves of them.

Later in Book I, as Milton prepares to describe the principals among
the fallen angels, he anticipates a time when these angels will
become worshipped as false gods. That worship will take the form
of 'gay religions full of pomp and gold' (372). Again, Milton is
implicitly associating the fallen angels with ritualised and elaborate
forms of worship.

As the fallen angels begin to build in Hell, they mine gold, and
Milton again shows his contempt for ostentation and display: 'Let
none admire / That riches grow in Hell; that soil may best / Deserve
the precious bane' (690–2).

Gold, the basis of the sort of ornamentation found in non-Puritan
churches, has its roots, according to Milton, in Hell. And the leader
of the fallen angels who ransack the earth for treasure is Mammon.
He is characterised by Milton as the sort of false priest so despised
by the Puritans:

CONTEXT

There are two
chapters in *A
Companion to
Milton* (Wiley
Blackwell, 2003)
that may shed
further light on
this topic. One is
'Milton and
Puritanism' by N.
H. Keble, the
other 'Milton on
the Bible' by
Regina M.
Schwarz.

CONTEXT

In 1649 Milton
wrote in
condemnation of
proposals which
would have
allowed Catholics
to stand for
Parliament in
Ireland: the short
title of that work
is *Observations on
the Articles of
Peace*, although
the full title
includes the words
'Irish Rebels and
Papists', and these
give a clear
indication of
where Milton's
sympathies lay.

PURITANISM AND CHRISTIANITY continued

CHECK THE BOOK

Satiric attacks on the clergy have a long history: they are, for example, prominent in Chaucer's *The Canterbury Tales*. His descriptions of the Prioress, the Monk, the Friar, the Summoner and the Pardoner all demonstrate Chaucer's keen sense of corruption in the Church.

CHECK THE BOOK

In the Prologue to his Tale the Pardoner confesses that, although his theme in preaching in church is always 'Radix malorum est cupiditas' (the love of money is the root of all evil), he tricks his congregation into giving him their goods: 'By this gaud [trick] have I wonne year by year / A hundred marks, since I was pardonere.'

His looks and thoughts
Were always downwards bent, admiring more
The riches of Heaven's pavement, trodden gold,
Than aught divine or holy else enjoyed
In vision beatific. (680–84)

Gold is mined from the beneath the surface of Earth, and Milton specifically locates Hell as beneath the Earth in Book III, line 322 when God refers to 'Heaven, or earth, or under earth in Hell'. Gold itself, therefore, is, by implication, a product of Hell.

The very building which the fallen angels erect, Pandemonium, is 'built like a temple' (713), almost the final negative reference in this opening Book to the kinds of religious observations of which Milton so vehemently opposed. The very last reference is in line 795 (this kind of attack does not figure so prominently in Book II), in which the meeting of the fallen angels is described as a 'conclave', a reference to the secret meeting of Roman Catholic cardinals at which a new Pope is elected.

LEADERSHIP AND AUTHORITY

Paradise Lost is a political poem as well being as a religious one. It was written after the revolution which led to the execution of Charles I and after what seemed to have been the failure of the Commonwealth under the leadership of Oliver Cromwell. Questions about who should be in charge, on what basis leadership should be established and what sort of leadership was displayed by those in charge were very pertinent issues for debate in the 1660s, so soon after the Restoration of the monarchy.

Satan's leadership receives the greatest share of attention in the opening two Books of *Paradise Lost*, but readers are simultaneously aware of the over-arching leadership and authority of God, even though he does not actually appear in this section of the poem. Furthermore, although the focus of these first two Books is on Satan and his claims for leadership of the fallen angels, the first Book starts with 'Man' (1), with 'Christ' (4), with 'Moses' (as the author of Genesis) (8), and with 'God' (12). Even in this very opening, we are told that Satan's claims are falsely based: his aim is 'To set himself in glory above his peers' (39).

Satan's claims are undercut throughout these first two Books. As Satan begins his first stirrings in Hell, the **narrator** points out that such movement is possible only because God allows it: 'the will / And high permission of all-ruling Heaven / Left him at large to his own dark designs' (Book I: 210–12). Satan and Beëlzebub believe that they have effected this change themselves: 'Both glorying to have scaped the Stygian flood /As gods, and by their own recovered strength, / Not by the sufferance of supernal Power' (Book I: 239–41).

The reader is told that Satan has been cast out from Heaven for pride (Book I: 36, 58, 572 and 603) and ambition (Book I: 41). Furthermore, the war in Heaven is described as an 'impious war' (43), a 'battle proud' (43) and a 'vain attempt' (44) before Satan even speaks.

The reader is invited to ask what the basis is for Satan assuming leadership in Hell. We learn that he has led the revolt by the rebel angels in Heaven (and this is never disputed in the poem as a whole: when Raphael gives his account of the war to Adam later in *Paradise Lost*, he re-affirms that Satan led the rebels). But does this explain why he should be leader in Hell? His military leadership is repeatedly emphasised in the opening Book (he is a 'Leader of … armies' in 272, a 'general' in 337, a 'commander' in 358 and 589, and a 'chief' in 525) but the effect of the Book as a whole is to present such militarism in a negative light.

Satan and his followers characterise themselves as having warred against an oppressive ruler: Satan describes God as holding 'the tyranny of Heaven' (124), and later attributes the basis of God's rule simply to custom and tradition:

> he who reigns
> Monarch in Heaven, till then as one secure
> Sat on his throne, upheld by old repute,
> Consent or custom. (637–41)

CONTEXT

Milton's own views on armed conflict were complex. He wrote the sonnet 'When the Assault was Intended to the City' in 1642 when it seemed likely that the Royalist army would take London. The poem shows him chiding the Royalist commanders for considering attacking the house of a poet. This somewhat humorous reaction to the military gave way to his working on behalf of Oliver Cromwell, whose own army had brought him to power. By 1660, when the monarchy had been restored, it was evident that real power could not be sustained by military might alone.

CHECK THE BOOK

The development of Milton's thinking is shown in his 1652 sonnet which begins 'Cromwell, our chief of men', which shows Milton's fear that military victory had not brought religious toleration. Antonia Fraser took the opening line of this sonnet as the title of her 1973 biography of Cromwell (Phoenix, 2001).

CHECK THE POEM

For a comparison with Satan taking on the task of corrupting mankind and his manner of doing it, read Book III lines 227 ff. on the Son's offer to redeem mankind, and the humility which he shows.

CHECK THE POEM

See Book VI lines 824–34 for an account of what actually caused Heaven to shake.

Similarly, Beëlzebub asserts that God's supremacy rests on 'strength, or chance or fate' (Book I: 133), and later (Book II: 325 ff.) characterises God as King, Emperor and Conqueror. For Mammon, God remains 'Our envied Sovereign' (Book II: 244). Satan argues at the beginning of Book II that his position in Hell, in contrast, is more secure than that of God, because nobody would envy the ruler of Hell (25–30).

Even when the fallen angels appear to be using positive terms to describe God, such as 'Almighty' (Book I: 259) and 'Omnipotent' (Book I: 272) these terms are loaded with irony. When they are repeated in Book II lines 144 and 198 the scorn of the speakers is intensified, as the words are used as adjectives rather than as nouns.

Yet Satan becomes a king himself. In Book II Satan takes on the task of corrupting mankind, the **narrator** describes him as speaking 'with monarchal pride' (428), 'raised / Above his fellows' (42–8), and, as he leaves Hell, he meets Death, who wears a 'kingly crown' (673).

Milton implies that monarchy and the perception of monarchy and unfounded hierarchies begin in Hell. Satan displays that 'monarchal pride' (Book II: 398), after the fallen angels have voted on the best course of action. Furthermore, although Beëlzebub proposes electing someone to take on the ruin of mankind (Book II: 413–16), that election does not take place. In a parallel fashion, Satan claims at an earlier point (Book II: 18–19) that the fixed law of Heaven made him the leader of the fallen angels, and that they chose him freely: there is no evidence for this claim in the account in Book V of the war in Heaven. In Book I the call to the assembly at Pandemonium goes out to 'By place or choice the worthiest' (759), but it is not clear how such appointments or elections took place.

Satan's claim for leadership rests on what he did in that war, yet his account is shown to be flawed. Satan claims innumerable forces of spirits followed him (Book I: 101) and that revolt emptied Heaven (Book I: 632–3), but Death gives a very different calculation of the size of the rebellion (692). Satan also claims that his rebellion shook the throne of God (105), but the later account of the war in Heaven gives the lie to this claim also.

As further evidence of the way in which Milton contrives to make the origins of the monarchy and the aristocracy grounded in Hell, the readers should note that Satan and his followers constantly invoke the names of the orders of angels. This is a complex topic because there is little biblical authority for the names of different kinds of angel. Nevertheless, there is considerable interest in angelology (the study of angels and their hierarchies) among theologians, and there are many books, articles and websites on this subject.

Perhaps it is most important to note that the orders of angels are usually presented as representing different functions and roles undertaken by the angels, rather than as a hierarchical system which gives one kind of angel a superior status to another. It is the fallen angels, especially Satan, who invoke these titles in a hierarchical way, to remind themselves of what they see as their lost status.

Notions of status permeate these first two Books. When the fallen angels change size as they enter Pandemonium, this affects only the unnamed rebels: the leaders of the hierarchy stay the same size (792–7): something comparable happens in Book II when Death increases his size to assert his superiority over Satan (705–6).

Satan's volunteering to take on the ruin of mankind might look like the act of a leader, and it involves him acting alone, as heroes often do, not least in **epic narratives**. It is commonplace to find that the leader bases his (for it is usually a man) claim for leadership on some individual act of bravery, undertaken for the benefit of his people. In the Anglo-Saxon epic *Beowulf*, the hero goes even further and carries out an act of individual bravery for a race other than his own. Yet in Book II Satan justifies his leadership and his monarchy by volunteering to leave Hell and his 'subjects', which is, to say the least, ironic. It is more usual in epics for the heroes to go on journeys before they are appointed as rulers.

Despite all the apparent resentment on the part of the fallen angels of their worship of God, the debate in Hell concludes with their worship of Satan: 'Towards him they bend / With awful reverence

> **CONTEXT**
>
> The standard hierarchical ordering of the ranks placed angels into three degrees, or 'choirs', each consisting of three ranks: Seraphim, Cherubim, Thrones; Dominions, Virtues, Powers; Principalities, Archangels, Angels. Satan uses some of these titles at the beginning of the debate in Book II.

 QUESTION

Do heroes have to act alone? If so, why should that be?

prone; and as a god / Extol him equal to the highest in Heaven' (Book II: 477–9).

To be worshipped as a god is surely the pinnacle of leadership, and, at this point in Book II Satan's state is described as being 'God-like imitated' (511). This takes the reader back to Book I when in lines 392 ff., Satan gathers his principal followers in a **parody** of Christ's disciples. The description of these twelve fallen angels at that point makes it clear that they are to become worshipped by people as gods later in history: Satan does not become the object of human worship (at least as far as Milton knew), but he does have angel worshippers in Book II.

At the debate in Book II, Satan sits 'exalted' (5), physically sitting on a higher level than the other fallen angels, a point which is reiterated at line 300. He achieves what the **narrator** calls 'that bad eminence' (5–6) because his wickedness merits it. But even Satan finds his status challenged, not by his fellow rebels, but by Death. Death claims to reign over Satan (698–9), a subversion of the hierarchy that conventionally exists between father and son. This subversion is continued when Sin describes Death as 'my son and foe' (804), but Sin herself, in a moment of supreme irony, chooses to obey her father, Satan, but, at the same time denies the obedience which she should show to God: 'Thou are my father, thou my author, thou / My being gavest me; whom should I obey / But thee, who follow?' (864–6). Following and obedience are essential to the creation of a leader, and Sin pledges her obedience here to Satan, rather than to God.

Through the theme of leadership and control, therefore, Milton implies that obedience to God should always take priority over all other forms of obedience, including obedience to any form of earthly rule. It is self-evident that Sin is following the wrong course by putting Satan before God, but Milton believed that his fellow-countrymen were equally culpable in pledging their allegiance to the monarchy.

CHECK THE POEM

In 1655 a group of Piedmontese Protestants were massacred by the command of the Catholic Duke of Savoy, and Milton responded by composing an impassioned sonnet calling for the vengeance of God against those who had perpetrated this outrage. The sonnet is available online under its title 'On the Late Massacre at Piedmont'. Go to **www.sonnets.org** and type 'Milton' into the search box.

LANGUAGE AND STYLE

The language of *Paradise Lost* has provoked much criticism (see also **Critical perspectives: Critical history**). There has been a widespread misconception that John Milton's language is 'difficult', and that he wrote with a **syntax** and a diction closer to Latin than to English.

This has taken a long time to die out, even though it has, in part, been challenged by statistical surveys of Milton's language, which have compared his usage with that of other writers. However, these surveys can provide only a limited insight into Milton's practice in his poetry, where it is impossible to discriminate between a strangeness of word order arising from the imitation of another language, and the kinds of inversion which are a necessary consequence of the decision to write in verse.

The following lyric, for example, from Shakespeare's *As You Like It* (II.5.1–8), illustrates some of the ways in which conventional word order changes in the transformation from prose to verse:

Under the greenwood tree
Who loves to lie with me,
And turn his merry note
Unto the sweet bird's throat,
Come hither, come hither, come hither:
Here shall he see
No enemy
But winter and rough weather.

There is a considerable difference between the ordering of the words in this lyric and that in a prose passage expressing the same idea. Yet no critic has suggested that Shakespeare was wrenching the English language; nor has anyone complained of the strangeness of the word order in the following passage from *Macbeth* (II.2.61–3):

'this my hand will rather
The multitudinous seas incarnadine,
Making the green one red.'

CONTEXT

The English language, like the Germanic languages from which it is derived, relies upon word-order to make its syntactic or grammatical distinctions: thus 'The man bit the dog' means something different from 'The dog bit the man' even though the words are the same. In Latin, however, word order is much less significant since the endings of words indicate which is the thing acting and the thing acted upon. A Latinate syntax, therefore would be one in which the usual word order of English was disrupted – 'Him the Almighty power / Hurled headlong' (Book I: 44–5) rather than 'The Almighty power hurled him headlong'.

CONTEXT

Sir John Cheke
(1514–57) was
opposed to
vocabulary drawn
from Latin and, in
his translation of
Matthew's gospel,
'crucified' became
'crossed' and
'centurion'
became
'hundreder'.

despite the fact that it includes 'incarnadine', a verb of Shakespeare's
own invention, based upon a Latin root. We accept that 'incarnadine'
has been separated from 'will' for reasons of emphasis and **metre**, and
that 'the green' probably means 'the green sea'. Detractors of Milton's
style have too rarely exercised such acceptance.

It would be possible to attempt a statistical survey of certain
features of Milton's poetic style which were felt to be unnatural to
the English language, and to compare the incidence of these features
in the work of a number of writers. Yet such a survey would
probably prove little. Some instances of disrupted word order will
seem particularly successful, as in the cases from Shakespeare cited
above, whereas a different example of precisely the same disruption
will seem discordant. Furthermore, it may not be possible in every
case to state with certainty whether or not 'normal' or
'conventional' word order has been followed by Milton. For
example, Satan's speech at the beginning of Book II includes the
following: 'From this descent / Celestial virtues rising will appear /
More glorious and more dread than from no fall' (14–16).

CONTEXT

In his Preface to
Lyrical Ballads,
Wordsworth
explained that:
'[*Lyrical Ballads*]
was published as
an experiment …
to ascertain, how
far, by fitting to
metrical
arrangement a
selection of the
real language of
men in a state of
vivid sensation,
that sort of
pleasure and that
quantity of
pleasure may be
imparted, which a
Poet may
rationally
endeavour to
impart.'

If we were looking for examples of adjectives following nouns
rather than, as is usual, preceding them, we might feel that this
passage yielded no evidence: it seems quite conventional in its use of
adjectives. However, it is at least arguable that the first eight words
in this passage could be read either as 'from this fall, Heavenly
angels will appear rising', as 'from this fall, rising celestial virtues
will appear', or as 'from this celestial fall, rising angels will appear'.
The lines can thus be read to include two instances of the inversion
of adjective and noun, one instance, or none at all.

The comparison between the language of Milton and that of
Shakespeare may become further skewed in Shakespeare's favour,
because most of Shakespeare's work is in the form of drama rather
than poetry, and drama needs, of necessity, to be more immediately
accessible (see **Critical approaches: Satan and drama**). A
comparison between the language of Milton and that of another
poet, William Wordsworth (1770–1850), may provide a fairer
evaluation of like with like. The opening Book of Wordsworth's
poem *The Prelude* (1805), includes these lines:

O welcome friend!
A captive greets thee, coming from a house
Of bondage, from yon city's walls set free,
A prison where he hath been long immured.
Now I am free, enfranchised and at large,
May fix my habitation where I will.
What dwelling shall receive me, in what vale
Shall be my harbour, underneath what grove
Shall I take up my home, and what sweet stream
Shall with its murmurs lull me to my rest? (5–14)

Wordsworth's language is closer to our own by some one hundred and fifty years, and so should seem more familiar. Moreover, in his Preface to the *Lyrical Ballads* (1800), Wordsworth set out to fashion a poetic diction close to the language of ordinary people, and, if he carried out that project successfully, his language should be very accessible.

Despite the fact that in *The Prelude*, Wordsworth was writing a little later and for a different audience from that of the *Lyrical Ballads*, the above extract serves to demonstrate that even a poet striving for simplicity, as Wordsworth did, may find that poetic diction has to be more heightened than the language of everyday conversation. In point of fact, in this short extract, we find some complex and unfamiliar diction in 'immured', 'enfranchised' and 'habitation'.

What may not be sufficiently appreciated, in all the emphasis on Milton's Latinate diction, is his use of graphic English words. For example, in the description of the creation of gold in Book I (lines 700–7), he employs some evocative terms which are all the more effective because they have been part of the English language for a long time, words such as 'dross', 'scummed' and 'sluiced'.

Milton exercises great care in his selection of language, frequently exploiting opportunities for multiple meaning. For example, in Book I he describes an architectural feature as 'Built like a temple, where pilasters round / Were set' (713–14). This seems an odd expression, given that pilasters are rectangular, and yet what Milton is doing is drawing the reader's attention to this apparent **paradox**

> **CONTEXT**
>
> 'Dross' and 'scum' are both words recorded in the earliest periods of the English language, and show the links between Old English (that stage of English before the Norman Conquest in 1066, sometimes referred to as 'Anglo-Saxon') and the Germanic languages on which it was based. 'Sluice' comes into the language slightly later, brought from French by the Norman invaders.

CHECK THE BOOK

Thomas Corns includes an excellent chapter on 'Milton's English' in *A Companion to Milton* (Wiley Blackwell, 2003), which charts the debates over Milton's language, especially the charge that it is Latinate.

CHECK THE NET

Milton's translation of verse ten of Psalm 84 reads: 'For one day in thy courts to be / Is better and more blest / Than in the joys of vanity / A thousand days at best'. The entire translation is available online at the Milton Reading Room – **www.dartmouth. edu** – as are the majority of other lesser known works by Milton mentioned in this section, including the 1668 version of *Paradise Lost.*

(line 713), and then resolving it in the line that follows (line 714), by extending the sentence so that it is read to mean 'like a temple, where pilasters were set round'. Similar instances of ambiguity are discussed in the **Detailed summaries** in relation to 'utter woe' (Book II: 87), 'cope' (Book I: 345) and 'partial' (Book II: 552). We might also note that he uses 'upsent' (Book I: 541) in one of the first recorded instances of the word, and, in contrast, that he is among the last writers to use these particular meanings for 'starve' (Book II: 600) and 'supply' (Book II: 834).

It is difficult not to be impressed by the range of Milton's vocabulary, especially as it relates to the range of his particular fields of knowledge – he is able to draw on detailed technical terms from architecture, from the sea and sailing, and from mining and foundry. Moreover, he reveals a detailed knowledge of the Bible and the Book of Common Prayer, not just in the biblical narratives he **alludes** to, but also in ways of phrasing. The line which is almost Satan's motto, for example, – 'Better to reign in Hell than serve in Heaven' (Book I: 263) – is, in its phrasing, drawn from Psalm 84, one of the Psalms which Milton translated in his youth (see Gordon Campbell, *John Milton, Complete English Poems, Of Education, Areopagitica*, p. 156); and the words of Sin to Satan (Book II: 868–70) are a direct **parody** of the words of the Creed.

Paradise Lost is also renowned for Milton's use of the **epic simile**, but it is possible to exaggerate its frequency. There are more epic similes in Book I than in Book II, even though the latter Book is longer. This is because Book I includes more description and fewer speeches than Book II, and this particular stylistic feature is more frequently associated with description. What is impressive about Milton's epic similes is the range of **tenors** he uses, drawn from the Bible (for example, Book I: 338), from classical legend (Book I: 197), and from his own contemporary experience (Book I: 287). Discussion of some specific examples of the epic simile can be found in the **Detailed summaries** in **Part Two** of these Notes.

BLANK VERSE

Paradise Lost is written in **blank verse**, which is distinguished by two features: the absence of rhyme, and the regularity of its rhythmic patterning. The typical line of a blank verse poem will consist of ten syllables, with stress on the even numbered syllables. This kind of line is called an **iambic pentameter**, and is exemplified by this line from the beginning of Book II:

His proud imaginations thus displayed.
˘   /   ˘ / ˘ / ˘   /   ˘   / (10)

Sometimes the same word will need to be pronounced differently in different lines because the blank verse rhythm requires it. For example, in this passage from Book I the Broadbent edition indicates how the individual words need to be read in order for the rhythm of the blank verse line to work:

> Thus they
> Breathing united force with fixèd thought
> Moved on in silence to soft pipes that charmed
> Their painful steps o'er the burnt soil; (559–62)

The word 'fixèd' has a stress on its second syllable, whereas 'charmed' in the next line does not. In this line from Milton's earlier poem *Comus,* the word 'charmed' needs to be pronounced 'charmèd' in order for the rhythm to work properly: 'The daughter of the Sun, whose charmèd cup …'

Blank verse became popular as the medium of many Elizabethan and Jacobean plays, including those of Christopher Marlowe and William Shakespeare, perhaps because it proved well suited to the needs of actors and audiences alike, being a form of verse relatively easy to speak and to follow.

In the edition of *Paradise Lost* published in 1668, Milton added an explanation of his decision to use blank verse (which he called 'English Heroic Verse'):

> The Measure is *English* Heroic Verse without Rime, as that of *Homer* in *Greek*, and *Virgil* in *Latin*; Rime being no necessary Adjunct or true Ornament of Poem or good Verse, in longer Works especially, but the Invention of a barbarous Age, to set off wretched matter and lame Meeter.

 CHECK THE NET

See the Darkness Visible website, a resource at the University of Cambridge, dedicated to the study of *Paradise Lost*, for further discussion of Milton's language – go to **www.christs.cam. ac.uk** and follow the link.

CHECK THE NET

Extracts from Surrey's version of the *Æneid* can be accessed via the Luminarium website – **www.luminarium. org**. Go to the section 'Renaissance' and click on 'Henry Howard'.

CONTEXT

Percy Bysshe Shelley (1792–1822) was a poet and a revolutionary thinker. He drowned shortly before his thirtieth birthday, but had, in his short life, produced a significant body of writing. Alfred, Lord Tennyson (1809–1892) was among the most revered of Victorian poets, and was Poet Laureate. He was also an admirer of the work of Shelley.

Milton is correct in that classical Latin and Greek verse did not use rhyme, and he may also have adopted blank verse for his **epic** because that was the form used by Henry Howard, Earl of Surrey (1517–47) in his version of Books II and IV of the *Æneid* (c. 1554), probably the first time that blank verse was used in English. This is an extract from Howard's translation of Book IV of the *Æneid*:

> Then from the seas the dawning gan arise.
> The sun once up, the chosen youth gan throng
> Unto the gates; the hayes so rarely knit,
> The hunting staves with their broad heads of steel,
> And of Massile the horsemen, forth they brake;

Blank verse became unfashionable in the later part of the seventeenth century, but it was revived by later poets including Wordsworth, Shelley, Keats and, most notably, Tennyson. It may be no coincidence that Milton was popular with the first three of these poets because he, like them, had revolutionary political views (see Wordsworth's sonnet beginning 'Milton, thou should'st be living at this hour'). Milton was also a model for Tennyson because, by Tennyson's time, there had been a popular return to the reading of religious poetry.

Milton's decision not to use rhyme might have been part of his wish to revive the roots of English poetry, which did not use rhyme as its basic principle, but instead used **alliteration** and rhythm. The extent to which alliteration still pervades everyday language is evidenced in such phrases as 'kith and kin' and 'time and tide'.

RHETORIC

Milton had a particular interest in language throughout his life, and, in particular, in the way in which language should be studied and taught. He attended St Paul's School in London, where the syllabus was somewhat unconventional for its time. The traditional basis of education in the medieval period had been the trivium (grammar, logic, and **rhetoric**), which had also been the foundation of classical education from Aristotle onwards. The teaching at St Paul's was based upon more radical principles derived from humanist thinking, which encouraged wide reading as a grounding for good use of language, rather than artificial exercises.

It may well have been this more liberal notion of education that led to his dispute with his tutor at Cambridge, and Milton's own views on education, as represented in his writing on the subject. His pamphlet *Of Education* was published in 1644 and reprinted in 1673, and his tutoring of his nephews was rooted in this humanist tradition. He had himself continued his own education through an extensive programme of reading during the time between his leaving university and his setting out on his continental tour (see **Background: Milton's life and works**).

Milton was anxious to discriminate between logic and rhetoric, as were some of his contemporaries and friends. He shared their suspicion of the flourishes and subtleties of rhetoric, which were seen as being associated with the old ways of Roman Catholicism, designed to mystify secular people. Milton continually advocated the promotion of poetry as an educational medium, and the denigration of rhetoric itself. Although the word 'rhetoric' does not occur in *Paradise Lost*, it is there both in his earlier work, *Comus*, and in the later poem *Paradise Regained*, and in both it is used negatively.

In *Comus*, the Lady chastises the tempter Comus with these words: 'Enjoy your deer Wit, and gay Rhetorick / That hath so well been taught her dazling fence, / Thou art not fit to hear thy self convinc't.' In *Paradise Regained* Satan's state after having failed to tempt Christ, is described in these terms:

> Perplex'd and troubl'd at his bad success
> The Tempter stood, nor had what to reply,
> Discover'd in his fraud, thrown from his hope,
> So oft, and the perswasive Rhetoric
> That sleek't his tongue, and won so much on Eve,
> So little here, nay lost; but Eve was Eve,
> This far his over-match, who self deceiv'd
> And rash, before-hand had no better weigh'd
> The strength he was to cope with, or his own: (Book IV: 1–9)

Late in his life in 1672, Milton published his *Artis Logicae* ('Art of Logic'). This work, composed in Latin, again espouses the humanist attempts to redefine the study of logic, to separate it from rhetoric,

CHECK THE NET
Aristotle (384 BC–322 BC) was a Greek philosopher and teacher who wrote on a number of different subjects. His *Rhetoric*, and a range of his other works, is available online in translation from **http://classics.mit.edu**

CHECK THE NET

A good introduction to Milton's views on education, rhetoric, logic and poetry can be found in the notes which accompany the online version of *Of Education* at the Milton Reading Room website. There is also a fascinating article by Jean E. Graham, 'Virgin Ears: Silence, Deafness, and Chastity in Milton's *Maske*' in *Milton Studies 36* (1998): 1–17, which gives further examples of Milton's attitude to rhetoric.

QUESTION

What examples can you find in Books I and II of Satan employing rhetoric?

to counter the orthodox Aristotelian approach to the trivium, and to reorganise the teaching of the arts.

Satan and Machiavelli

One particular aspect of the language of persuasion is worth mentioning here in connection with Satan's **rhetoric**, and that is the connection between Satan and Machiavelli.

The Italian diplomat and writer Niccolò Machiavelli (1469–1527) exerted a special influence on Renaissance thinking on politics, especially through his work *The Prince*, published after his death, in 1532. The work is a textbook on how to succeed in politics, and gained its author a posthumous reputation as an advocate of ruthlessness. Its promotion of violence as a means of achieving political ends led to it being banned by the Roman Catholic Church in the middle of the sixteenth century.

As an indication of the extent to which the reputation of Machiavelli was part of the popular culture of Milton's time, one need go no further than the play *The Jew of Malta* (1592) by Christopher Marlowe, in which the character Machiavel speaks the Prologue, in order to underline the wickedness of the characters to be introduced in the play. Marlowe himself (1564–93) was arrested on charges of atheism in 1593.

Milton's political thinking, especially on republicanism, may well have owed much to the theories of Machiavelli, but the more significant debt for students of *Paradise Lost* may have been in terms of the role of language in politics. Machiavelli knew that persuasion was important, but he also argued that it was insufficient on its own as a mechanism to effect political change. In Chapter 6 of *The Prince* he writes:

> Hence it is that all armed prophets have conquered, and the unarmed ones have been destroyed. Besides the reasons mentioned, the nature of the people is variable, and whilst it is easy to persuade them, it is difficult to fix them in that persuasion. And thus it is necessary to take such measures that, when they believe no longer, it may be possible to make them believe by force.

In Chapter 19 he gives a specific example:

> [Severus] persuaded the army in Sclavonia, of which he was
> captain, that it would be right to go to Rome and avenge the
> death of Pertinax, who had been killed by the praetorian soldiers;
> and under this pretext, without appearing to aspire to the throne,
> he moved the army on Rome, and reached Italy before it was
> known that he had started.

There is much that is Machiavellian in Satan's tactics, as represented
by Milton in *Paradise Lost*. He is skilful in his persuasive powers,
but also knows that words need to be followed by actions.

One critic in particular has noted this resemblance. Barbara
Riebling, writing in the *Renaissance Quarterly* in 1996 says: 'When
first introduced in Books one and two of *Paradise Lost*, Satan seems
to bear a striking resemblance to Machiavelli's ideal prince –
impetuous, confident, courageous, and sly' ('Milton on Machiavelli:
Representations of the State in "Paradise Lost"', Volume 49, p. 574).

USE OF BIBLICAL REFERENCES

The Bible presents the story of the beginnings of all things, a story
which, as far as Milton was concerned, took precedence over all the
stories contained in classical legends and all possible subjects for
classical **epics**. Milton relies heavily upon the Bible as a source and
so it is unsurprising that we should find a wealth of biblical
references in his poem. However, Milton also deploys these
references in order to make a point about the status of the story that
he is telling.

For example, Milton makes no attempt to suppress the notion that
large numbers of angels fell with Satan (this is particularly the case
in Book I). The catalogue of named fallen angels is extensive, and is
followed by a description of the throng of unnamed angels.
However, Milton diminishes the effect of all these numbers by
undermining their status, comparing them to a swarm of insects in
Book I lines 767–92.

In Book I (from line 305 onwards) Milton refers to the story of the
parting of the Red Sea. This story, from the book of Exodus, comes

**CHECK
THE BOOK**
For the influence of
Machiavelli on
Milton's political
thinking and his
views on rhetoric,
see the studies by
Z. S. Fink, *The
Classical
Republicans*
(Northwestern
University Press,
1962) and V. Kahn,
*Machiavellian
Rhetoric: From the
Counter-
Reformation to
Milton* (Princeton
University Press,
1994).

near the beginning of the narrative of the escape of the chosen people of Israel to the Promised Land. However, Milton does not simply refer to this biblical story as part of his **epic simile** – he deliberately mixes it with the more conventional, classical references to Vallombrosa and Etruria. He allots two and a half lines to the comparison with classical epic and ten lines to the reference to the biblical story. A few lines later, Milton refers to the plague of locusts, again from Exodus. Both of these biblical references emphasise the power of God, and God's ability to rescue his believers in circumstances which appear hopeless. Perhaps more significantly, they assert the supremacy of a Christian God over the gods of classical legend.

IMAGES OF THE SUN

Hell is frequently described in terms of images of the sea and of night (see also **Themes: Uncertainty and instability**). However, on three occasions in the opening two Books, Milton employs an image that depends upon a specific contrast, that of the sun shrouded by clouds. The first is as a **simile** for Satan's towering but dimmed appearance:

> as when the sun new risen
> Looks through the horizontal misty air
> Shorn of his beams, or from behind the moon,
> In dim eclipse, disastrous twilight sheds
> On half the nations, and with fear of change
> Perplexes monarchs. (Book I: 594–9)

Here, at a relatively early point in the epic, Milton is making the point that Satan, whilst retaining some remnants of his former glory and light, has now, through his fall, become darkened like an eclipse, and become potentially fearful. His appearance is compared to that of the sun when it cannot be fully seen, either partially hidden in mist or by an eclipse.

The second, similar simile occurs as part of Mammon's speech in Book II, urging the fallen angels not to fear Hell:

> How oft amidst
> Thick clouds and dark doth Heaven's all-ruling sire

Choose to reside, his glory unobscured,
And with the majesty of darkness round
Covers his throne, from whence deep thunders roar,
Mustering their rage, and Heaven resembles Hell?
As he our darkness, cannot we his light
Imitate when we please? (263–70)

This clever piece of false logic suggests that the rebel angels, now cast into darkness, might regain their former light, just as the sun, if hidden by cloud, does not become permanently darkened. His argument is that the sun may be temporarily darkened by cloud during a thunderstorm, making the sun (Heaven) seem as dismal as Hell: therefore, he goes on, if the sun can be darkened, then Hell can become light. The phrase 'the majesty of darkness' is especially telling and effective.

The third image of sun and cloud is a description of the atmosphere, which follows the debate in Hell:

As, when from mountain tops the dusky clouds
Ascending, while the north wind sleeps, o'erspread
Heaven's cheerful face, the louring element
Scowls o'er the darkened landscape snow or shower,
If chance the radiant sun, with farewell sweet,
Extend his evening beam, the fields revive,
The birds their notes renew, and bleating herds
Attest their joy, that hill and valley rings. (Book II: 488–95)

Here the implication is that the false optimism generated by the debate gives the same illusion of revival to the fallen angels as does a single ray of the sun peeping through the clouds. There is irony here in the beauty of the image of the countryside, a beauty which is as far removed as possible from the situation of the rebel angels in Hell, and serves only to reinforce how false these small rays of hope are for them.

These three versions of a single common image serve to draw attention to the great divide which now exists between the place occupied by the fallen angels – a realm of uncertainty, darkness and unpredictability – and the natural world of sun, cloud, evening and

 CHECK THE BOOK

Eclipses were greatly feared by many people in this period. See, for example, the speech by the Duke of Gloucester in Shakespeare's *King Lear* Act I Scene 2: 'These late eclipses in the sun and moon portend no good to us.'

QUESTION

Frequently used images in these opening Books, in addition to the references to the sun and the sea, are those that focus on mining and foundry – see, for example, Book I lines 700–7. What effect do these images have?

CHECK THE BOOK

The **soliloquy** by the king at the beginning of Shakespeare's *Richard III*, and that which closes Act I Scene 2 are particularly worthy of study. In the second of these soliloquies, Richard, having wooed a woman whose husband he has murdered, addresses the audience in this fashion: 'Was ever woman in this humour woo'd? / Was ever woman in this humour won? / I'll have her; but I will not keep her long.'

morning. In our world we know that clouds will pass and that the night will give way to the morning. For the rebel angels, such certainty has gone.

SATAN AND DRAMA

There has been considerable critical interest in the figure of Satan in *Paradise Lost*, and in the possibility that he may be the true hero of the epic (see also **Critical perspectives**). Milton's nephew, Edward Phillips, asserted that it was Milton's original intention to write a tragic drama on the subject of the fall (see **Note on the text**). The attractiveness of Satan and the genesis of *Paradise Lost* as a drama are to some extent interwoven. It is a critical commonplace that, in drama, the audience is led to sympathise with and believe in the first voice they hear, especially if that voice speaks directly to the audience. In his book *Engagement with Knavery* (Duke University Press, 1986), R. C. Jones demonstrates how this principle operates in Renaissance plays such as Shakespeare's *Richard III*.

One reason why there is any case for regarding Satan as the hero of the poem is that we learn his version of events first and, by the end of Book II, we have received only his partial account of the war in Heaven.

One characteristic of Satan, which is particularly evident in the opening two Books of *Paradise Lost*, is his desire to rouse his fallen troops; to do this, he may well need to paint for them a more positive picture of what they have just experienced than is strictly true. S. A. J. Bradley, in the introduction to his translation of *Genesis B* (see **Note on the text**), says of the relationship between *Genesis B* and *Paradise Lost*: 'Both poets, as a direct consequence of opting for an epic heroic genre, risk counterproductively investing the rebel angel with an admirable dignity and heroic appeal which are inherent in the traditional diction and manner of the genre' (*Anglo-Saxon Poetry*, Everyman, 1982, p. 12). We should note Bradley's reference here to the 'opting', that is, making a choice: it is all too easy to forget that *Paradise Lost* is the product of much deliberate choice on Milton's part. Bradley goes on to compare the presentation of Satan in both poems with that of the Anglo-Saxon hero, Beowulf, and of Byrhtnoth, hero of the *Battle of Maldon*. One feature of the latter is that Byrhtnoth is defiant in the face of what seems to be certain defeat, and this defiance gives rise to a stirring turn of speech. For example (from Bradley's prose translation in *Anglo-Saxon Poetry*, p. 521):

> Do you hear, sea-wanderer, what this nation says? They will give you spears as tribute, the poison-tipped javelin and ancient swords, those warlike accoutrements which will profit you nothing in battle. Seamen's spokesman, report back again; tell your people much more distasteful news: that here stands a worthy earl with his troop of men who is willing to defend this his ancestral home, the country of Aethelraed, my lord's nation and land. The heathens shall perish in battle. It seems to me too despicable that you should take to your ships with our riches, unfought, now that you have intruded this far hither into our country. Not so smoothly shall you get gold. First point and edge shall sort things out between us, the fierce exchange of fighting, before we pay tribute.

This kind of expression is known as **flyting**. It is found frequently in Anglo-Saxon poetry and is also a characteristic of the style of the Elizabethan dramatist Christopher Marlowe, who deployed blank verse with great expertise in many of his plays. Satan's defiant words to Death in Book II of *Paradise Lost* can be described as an instance of flyting: 'Retire, or taste thy folly, and learn by proof, / Hell-born, not to contend with spirits of Heaven' (686–7).

Drama, especially that of Marlowe and of his contemporary Shakespeare, operates through an interchange of dialogue and soliloquy, public scenes and private scenes. In Books I and II of *Paradise Lost*, all the scenes are public, and we find no instance of a soliloquy, which is often more revealing of the true feelings of a character than the dialogue. However, Satan does have later soliloquies, which do much to undercut whatever initial impression we may have formed of his valour.

 CHECK THE POEM

For an example of one of Satan's later soliloquies, see the speech he addresses to the sun at the beginning of Book IV (lines 33–113), where he admits that his revolt against God was wrong.

It would be wrong to place too much emphasis on the dramatic qualities of *Paradise Lost*, because it is a poem, despite its dramatic origins (see **Note on the text**). However, there is one aspect of the difference between drama and **epic** poetry that readers must be aware of, and that is the difference between reading a poem and watching a play.

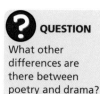

QUESTION

What other differences are there between poetry and drama?

When watching a play, the members of the audience must receive and interpret what is happening at a single sitting. They cannot interrupt the action and ask for explanation or for difficult scenes to be replayed. Thus, if the meaning of a particular word is obscure, the audience will have to ignore it, forget it, or hope that the general context will carry them through to understanding. In reading, however, there is a real danger that any word which has an obscure meaning will cause readers to stop and to turn for help outside the text. This may well have the unfortunate effect of making the text seem more difficult than it really is, and it will almost certainly inhibit the flow of the narrative. It is therefore important that readers of *Paradise Lost* try very hard to keep reading, perhaps noting words which are not clear in meaning, but not interrupting their reading to look them up immediately. This will help to keep the drama of Milton's great work alive.

THE ROLE OF THE NARRATOR

There is another difference between drama and a written text which merits consideration. Most dramas tell their narratives entirely through the interchange between characters, and relatively few employ the device of the **narrator**. However, in *Paradise Lost*, as in many other written texts, the narrator plays a crucial role both in moving the story onward and in shaping the reactions of the readers. This is particularly the case in Books I and II, where the only characters we meet are the fallen angels Sin, Death and Chaos. In these circumstances we might be in danger of being in total sympathy with the forces of evil, were it not for the narrator, who intervenes, for example, to point out the vanity and falseness of what is being said in the debate at the beginning of Book II. (See also **Detailed summaries – Book I Lines 588–669** in **Part Two** of these Notes.) Indeed, so significant is this narrative voice that we may need to reflect upon whether Satan's really is the first voice we hear in the poem, or whether we have already learned to attend to the narrator before Satan speaks for the first time.

The narrator is also Milton himself, and that is very significant at the opening of the epic, where the narrator/Milton seeks divine assistance in the writing of the poem:

> what in me is dark
> Illumine, what is low raise and support;
> That to the highth of this great argument
> I may assert eternal providence,
> And justify the ways of God to men. (Book I: 22–6)

Milton is placing himself in the line of divinely-inspired writers or prophets which, according to lines 6–10, goes back as far as Moses. This direct equation between the narrator and Milton occurs only relatively rarely in *Paradise Lost*, and always at the very beginning of a Book; at the beginning of Book VIII Milton renews his prayer for inspiration; at the beginning of Book IX he laments the fact that he must relate the tragedy of the fall of mankind; and at the beginning of Book III he amplifies a single word in Book I line 22 ('dark') to a full lament on his blindness. Each of these personal interventions by Milton is characterised by the inclusion of the word 'I', and the lament on his blindness, the most personal passage in the entire epic, uses the words 'I' or 'me' more than ten times.

It has been noted before that these first two Books include many negative references to God. In the face of all these negative views, the voice of the narrator has a vital role to play. That voice is not simply there to set the scene at the beginning of Book I or just to give voice to the passages of description found in both of the opening Books. It is there to redress the balance of opinions about God, and to remind readers quietly and with subtlety that everything which takes place within the poem happens solely through the permission of God. Two good examples of the power of this subdued narrative voice can be found in Book I, at lines 211–20 and lines 366–75.

QUESTION

If 'dark' in Book I line 22 refers to Milton's blindness, how else is darkness characterised in these first two Books?

CHECK THE BOOK

Read Book III lines 1–55, and consider whether Milton represents his blindness in an entirely negative way.

NARRATIVE FORM AND STRUCTURE

Paradise Lost does not follow a single continuous narrative line. In the true tradition of the **epic**, the story begins in the middle, *in medias res.*

CHECK THE BOOK

Homer's *Odyssey* and *Iliad*, Virgil's *Aeneid* and the *Inferno* from Dante's *Divine Comedy* all begin *in medias res.*

Events which occur before the opening of Book I are presented to the reader by various means, which include dreams, reminiscences and conversations, not all of which can be taken as entirely reliable. For example, in Books V and VI, the angel Raphael, sent down to Eden by God to enlighten and warn Adam, tells of the revolt of Satan against God and how, inspired by pride, ambition and envy, Satan seduced one tenth of the angelic host into following him. This account of the war in Heaven is in sharp contrast to the description provided by Satan in the early Books of the poem, and the difference between these two versions is a good example of why we cannot simply accept all accounts of the past as reliable.

Books I and II provide, in one single example, a microcosm of the narrative structure of the entire epic. In the poem as a whole we are to find that, like the fallen angels in the opening Books, we as readers have to live through uncertainty and instability (see **Themes: Uncertainty and instability**) as we learn not to trust the versions of the history of Heaven which are told to us. In Book II we have a debate in Hell presented to us, only to find that the speech by Beëlzebub does not represent his own viewpoint, as we might have thought, but is, in fact, the product of a plot between Satan and Beëlzebub to which we have not had access. Elsewhere in the epic we will find lengthy narratives which challenge the versions of events set out by the rebel angels in Books I and II; in Book II itself, the narrator himself provides just such a challenge with great economy by luring the readers into accepting what Beëlzebub says, only to reveal a very different version of events.

QUESTION

What other examples can you think of in literature of potentially unreliable narrators (one might be Nick Carraway in *The Great Gatsby* by F. Scott Fitzgerald, for example)?

A good sense of the structure of *Paradise Lost* as a whole can be gained from the **Synopsis** in **Part Two**.

SETTINGS

The principal location in the opening two Books of *Paradise Lost* is Hell, but in these Books Milton also introduces his readers to Heaven, to Eden, and to the uncharted territory between Hell and Eden.

Milton relies partly on his imagination in his description of these locations, but he also draws upon his interest in astronomy as he charts the relative positions of these regions. On his European tour in the late 1630s Milton visited Galileo, the distinguished Italian astronomer, imprisoned for adhering to his belief that the Earth was not the centre of the universe.

In his 1644 prose work, *Of Education*, Milton recommended that the ideal curriculum should include astronomy:

> And having thus passed the principles of arithmetic, geometry, astronomy, and geography with a general compact of physics, they may descend in mathematics to the instrumental science of trigonometry and from thence to fortification, architecture, engineering, or navigation.

Near the very beginning of Book I of *Paradise Lost*, Milton is careful in his location of Hell and Heaven:

> here their prison ordained
> In utter darkness, and their portion set
> As far removed from God and the light of Heaven
> As from the centre thrice to the utmost pole. (71–4)

Milton here identifies the Earth as the centre of the universe, and Heaven as 'the utmost pole'. Hell is three times as far away from Heaven as Earth is. At this point in the poem, Milton seems to be using an older system of beliefs than that of Galileo, and his intention may be to suggest that one consequence of the fall of man might be that Earth lost its position at the centre of the universe.

Milton, therefore, describes the relative positions of Heaven, Earth and Hell in this way: Hell is twice as far below Earth as Heaven is

CHECK THE BOOK
Galileo is specifically referred to by Milton in Book I of *Paradise Lost* (lines 286–91).

CHECK THE NET
The site *Shakespeare's Life and Times* – **http://internet shakespeare.uvic. ca** – has a section on Ideas which refers to Medieval and Renaissance theories on the universe (and includes contemporary maps) – go to 'Life & Times', 'Ideas', and 'The Universe'.

CONTEXT

There is further discussion of astronomy in the conversation between Adam and Raphael in Book VIII lines 119–68 of *Paradise Lost*.

above Earth, and Satan is able to make direct observation of these relative positions himself at the end of Book II:

> at leisure to behold
> Far off the empyreal Heaven, extended wide
> In circuit, undetermined square or round,
> With opal towers and battlements adorned
> Of living sapphire, once his native seat;
> And fast by hanging in a golden chain
> This pendent world, in bigness as a star
> Of smallest magnitude close by the moon. (1046–53)

Satan now sees that Heaven is so large that he cannot decide whether it is straight or curved, and he gains his first prospect of 'this pendent world' (confusingly, Milton means the universe, here, and not Earth). The universe hangs ('pendent') by a golden chain stretching from Heaven, and the **simile** tells us that its size in comparison to that of Heaven is comparable to the size of a tiny star set against the size of the moon.

The quotation above indicates something of the appearance of Heaven: jewel-like with its opal towers, sapphire battlements and the golden chain leading down to the universe. The phrase 'fast by' may indicate something of the stability of this system as well as the proximity of the universe to Heaven.

In contrast, in the description of Hell in Book II from line 587 onwards, Milton emphasises the instability of the environment ('dire hail, which on firm land / Thaws not', 589–91) and its forbidding appearance ('a frozen continent . . . dark and wild', 587–8).

Although Pandemonium may seem impressive, Milton describes its doors as 'brazen' (Book I: 724), and this adjective could carry the connotations of 'shameless' in Milton's time as it can now. Furthermore, although the architecture of Pandemonium includes 'golden architrave' (715), Milton makes it clear that this comes from a repulsive process: 'There stood a hill not far whose grisly top / Belched fire and rolling smoke' (670–1).

PART FOUR

CRITICAL PERSPECTIVES

READING CRITICALLY

This section provides a range of critical viewpoints and perspectives on *Paradise Lost* and gives a broad overview of key debates, interpretations and theories proposed since the poem was published. It is important to bear in mind the variety of interpretations and responses this text has produced, many of them shaped by the critics' own backgrounds and historical contexts.

No single view of the text should be seen as dominant – it is important that you arrive at your own judgements by questioning the perspectives described, and by developing your own critical insights. Objective analysis is a skill achieved through coupling close reading with an informed understanding of the key ideas, related texts and background information relevant to the text. These elements are all crucial in enabling you to assess the interpretations of other readers, and even to view works of criticism as texts in themselves. The ability to read critically will serve you well both in your study of *Paradise Lost* Books I and II, and in any critical writing, presentation, or further work you undertake.

ORIGINAL RECEPTION

The critical history of *Paradise Lost* is, unsurprisingly, a history of the reception of the poem as whole and not merely of its opening Books, and you will find that you need to have a sense of the scope of the entire epic in order to make sense of the criticism you read. You may find the **Synopsis** provided earlier in these Notes useful in this regard, together with the 'Argument' provided by Milton in the second edition of the poem.

The early editions of *Paradise Lost* sold well (particularly in comparison with Milton's first volume of poetry, *Poems 1645*), and Milton received royalty payments for his epic.

> **CONTEXT**
>
> *Poems 1645* (actually published in 1646) includes the English poems that Milton had written up to that time, plus a selection of poems in Latin. It includes *Lycidas*, and 'A Mask' (a work usually referred to as *Comus*), both of which had been published earlier. *Poems 1645* is available online at the Milton Reading Room – **www.dartmouth. edu/~milton/ reading_room**

CONTEXT

John Bunyan
(1628–88) began
*The Pilgrim's
Progress* whilst in
prison for
preaching without
a licence. The
book became one
of the most
widely-read and
influential of
Christian texts.

**CHECK
THE NET**

The website
Darkness Visible –
**www.christs.
cam.ac.uk/
darknessvisible** –
has a section on the
influence of
Paradise Lost, but
this tends to
concentrate on
imitations which
were successful. Less
successful imitators
included James
Thomson (1700–48)
and William Cowper
(1731–1800).

However, it was not until the publication in 1688 (after Milton's death) of a lavish and illustrated subscription edition of the poem that it could be claimed that *Paradise Lost* had achieved the status of an English classic. As the critic W. W. Robson remarked in a 1982 essay (in *The New Pelican Guide to English Literature*, ed. B. Ford, 1982, p. 243):

> In this present age, when it is rarely read except by scholars and literary specialists, we are likely to forget how popular *Paradise Lost* once was. It stood on the shelves of every respectable household, beside the Bible and *The Pilgrim's Progress.*

This very popularity, however, could be said to have worked against the liveliness of Milton's epic. It seems to have led to an unquestioning reverence of the poem on the part of many readers, and to the production of pale imitations of Milton's style by inferior poets, who failed to see that Milton is quite consciously placing himself at the end of a literary tradition.

Paradise Lost, in many respects, denies the validity of the **epic** poem (see **Literary background: The epic tradition**). However, Milton has never at any stage been totally beyond negative criticism, even on the part of his supporters. The essayist Joseph Addison (1672–1719), for example, wrote a series of papers on Milton for the *Spectator* in 1712 in which he finds the poet 'sublime', and yet this very assertion led Addison to defend and discuss aspects of *Paradise Lost* which he felt failed to live up to this quality.

Furthermore, the edition of *Paradise Lost* produced in 1732 by Richard Bentley (1662–1742) went as far as to amend those passages in the poem which the editor did not understand or did not like, on the grounds that these sections could not represent what the poet had intended.

Bentley justified some of his changes by claiming that Milton's original text was too shocking to have been what the poet intended; ironically, he thus emphasised one of the most conspicuous qualities of *Paradise Lost*. Milton undoubtedly intended his poem to shock and to challenge, and however eccentric Bentley's reading of the poem may be, it is arguable that Milton would have preferred

Bentley's active engagement with the text to the passive acquiescence which more traditional readers have accorded it. Milton, after all, continually advocated the need for an explicit faith which was constantly renewing itself by challenge and debate. The presence of recurring Milton controversies over the past two-and-a-half centuries has ensured that successive generations of serious readers have had their faith in Milton's epic enhanced by trial.

CRITICAL HISTORY

MILTON'S LANGUAGE

The language of *Paradise Lost* has been the subject of debate from Joseph Addison and Samuel Johnson onwards. Addison, as cited in *The Living Milton* (ed. F. Kermode, Routledge, 1960) argued that Milton 'has carried our language to a greater height than any of the English poets have ever done before or after him, and made the sublimity of his style equal to that of his sentiments' (p. 162).

However, he also complained on the very same page that 'our language sunk under him, and was unequal to that greatness of soul which furnished him with such glorious conceptions'. Johnson, more trenchantly, capped Addison's remark with this comment from *The Lives of the Most Eminent English Poets* (1783), claiming that Milton had 'formed his style by a perverse and pedantic principle. He was desirous to use English words with a foreign idiom … Of him, at last, may be said what [Ben] Jonson says of Spenser, that *he wrote no language*'. And of *Paradise Lost* as a whole, Samuel Johnson wrote a few pages earlier: '*Paradise Lost* is one of the books which the reader admires and lays down, and forgets to take up again. None ever wished it longer than it is. Its perusal is a duty rather than a pleasure.'

There can be a variety of reasons that lead a critic to write negatively of a poet, and Johnson's attacks owe as much to what he believed of Milton the man as to his views on poetry. The poet and critic T. S. Eliot shared Johnson's antipathy towards Milton the man, and he was not content simply to accuse Milton of having had a bad effect on later English poetry.

 CHECK THE NET
The Victorian Web – **www.victorianweb.org** – includes a section on Addison and the sublime (see 'Philosophy'). It contains a quotation from the *Spectator* 412 (1712) in which Addison explains that the greatness of a literary work, like the greatness of natural beauty, lies not just in 'the bulk of any single object but the largeness of a whole view considered as one entire piece. Such are the prospects of … a vast uncultivated desert, of huge heaps of mountains … where we are not struck with the novelty or beauty of the sight but with that rude kind of magnificence which appears in many of these stupendous works of nature'.

CONTEXT

T. S. Eliot (1888–1965) was born in the USA, but spent most of his life in England. He became one of the most celebrated poets of the twentieth century, as well as writing plays and works of literary criticism. His views on Milton and on seventeenth-century poetry became particularly influential.

QUESTION

What do you think Leavis might mean by the accusation that 'Milton has forgotten the English language'?

Eliot also claimed in *On Poetry and Poets* (Faber, 1957) that Milton lacked visual imagination, that his poetry gave priority to sound rather than to meaning, and that his language was remote: 'Every distortion of construction, the foreign idiom, the use of a word in a foreign way or with the meaning of the foreign word from which it is derived rather than the accepted meaning in English, every idiosyncrasy is a particular act of violence which Milton has been the first to commit' (p. 154).

In his second essay on Milton, Eliot shifted ground somewhat. Here he claimed that this remoteness was a mark of Milton's greatness, but the recantation was not allowed: the critic F. R. Leavis (1895–1978) continued the crusade against Milton which Eliot had begun by declaring that Milton's language was monotonous, pompous, laboured, pedantic and artificial. His attack in *Revaluation* (Chatto and Windus, 1936) was uncompromising:

> So complete, and so mechanically habitual, is Milton's departure from the English order, structure and accentuation that he often produces passages that have to be read through several times before one can see how they go, though the Miltonic mind has nothing to offer that could justify obscurity – no obscurity was intended: it is merely that Milton has forgotten the English language. (p. 53)

Leavis's attack upon Milton's language was based on several false premises. It tended to portray the 'grand style' of Milton's **epic** as unvarying and unwieldy, incapable of subtlety or delicacy, and incomparably poorer than the style of either Shakespeare or Spenser. The effect of the attack has been to prompt the publication of a number of excellent studies of *Paradise Lost*, each of which has demonstrated new intricacies in Milton's handling of the varied style of his epic. There are, undeniably, occasions when the style manifests complexity (a less emotive term than Leavis's 'obscurity'), but these occasions are always when a complex issue is being presented.

As Jonathan Richardson (1665–1745), an early commentator on *Paradise Lost*, observed in *Remarks on Milton's Paradise Lost*, the reader needs to be especially vigilant: 'A Reader of *Milton* must be

Always upon Duty; he is Surrounded with Sense, it rises in every Line, every Word is to the Purpose … he Expresses himself So Concisely, Employs Words So Sparingly, that whoever will Possess His Ideas must Dig for them, and Oftentimes pretty far below the Surface.'

Since this remark was made as long ago as 1734, it is odd that critics in the twentieth century should have continued to describe the language of *Paradise Lost* as mere music, as if Milton were using the sound of the words as an alternative for thought. Leavis's version of this line of attack, in *The Common Pursuit* (Chatto and Windus, 1952) is at least consistent with his other views on Milton: 'the man who uses words in this way has … no "grasp of ideas", and, whatever he may suppose, is not really interested in the achievement of precise thought of any kind' (p. 62).

C. S. Lewis, however, writing ostensibly in defence of Milton in *A Preface to Paradise Lost* (Oxford University Press, 1942) against the attacks of Eliot and Leavis, seems to come very close to finding Milton's language mere music himself: 'The epic diction, as Goethe said, is "a language which does your thinking and your poetising for you" … The conscious artistry of the poet is thus set free to devote itself wholly to the large-scale problems – construction, character drawing, invention; his *verbal* poetics have become a habit, like grammar and articulation' (p. 23).

The work of later critics such as Christopher Ricks, Stanley Fish and others (see **Critical history: Responses from Burden, Fish and Empson**) has demonstrated convincingly that Milton's epic diction is far from being a substitute for thought, and that it was no more subject to habit than his grammar or his use of **metre**. Although Milton employs impressive lists in his epic, these are not simply there to be magnificent. The scholarship of recent editors has indicated the extent to which Milton carefully constructs these catalogues either to undermine the reader's confidence in the character or situation being described, or to challenge the status of earlier epics.

> **CONTEXT**
>
> C. S. Lewis (1898–1963) was an Oxford academic who wrote extensively on medieval and Renaissance literature, as well as being the author of works of popular fiction, including *The Chronicles of Narnia*.

Lycidas is a poem of less than two hundred lines, which Milton contributed to a volume of poems published in 1638 in memory of his fellow-student Edward King who drowned in 1637. The poem gave Milton a vehicle to consider his own life in the light of King's premature death, and also, since King was to have taken Holy Orders, to comment on the nature of the contemporary clergy.

THE DEBATE ON GOD AND SATAN

Attacks on John Milton in the later twentieth century were almost exclusively concerned with *Paradise Lost*. Some critics wished that Milton had continued to write as he did in his 1637 poem *Lycidas*). They have done great service to the poem by posing questions and provoking responses which might otherwise never have been explicitly and systematically formulated. These attacks, mounted by some of the foremost writers of the century, have centred, oddly enough, on the very issues raised in Samuel Barrow's commendatory verses in the edition of 1674 (see **Note on the text**). Barrow's verse, written in Latin and less frequently quoted than that of Andrew Marvell, observes of Satan (in Gordon Campbell's translation): 'What a Lucifer ... hardly inferior to Michael himself!' It asks why any reader should read *Paradise Lost* without reading it in its entirety. These are, in effect, the main preoccupations of twentieth-century criticism of *Paradise Lost* – whether the reader can be expected to enjoy the entire poem, and whether Satan is presented too attractively.

Interest in the presentation of God and Satan in *Paradise Lost* is no new phenomenon, but it has proved a lively area of recent Milton study, in an age when **epic** language and epic conventions are unrecognised, and faith in God and a knowledge of the Bible cannot be taken for granted. The modern reader provides the ideal test for the validity of *Paradise Lost*.

Following William Blake's remark at the end of the eighteenth century in *The Marriage of Heaven and Hell* that 'The reason Milton wrote in fetters when he wrote of Angels and God, and at liberty when of Devils and Hell, is because he was a true Poet and of the Devil's party without knowing it', the character of Satan began to exercise a considerable influence on English fiction, especially through the villains of Gothic novels, who are often recognisable as Satan in all but name (see **Literary background: The Gothic tradition**).

In 1947, the critic A. J. A. Waldock systematised the feeling which had become popular through Gothic interpretations of Milton –

that Satan was an attractive figure, ill-deserving of his fate – in his book *Paradise Lost and Its Critics* (Cambridge University Press). Approaching the poem from the perspective of one well-versed in reading novels, Waldock argued that Milton had been so successful in his description of a powerful and attractive Satan in Books I and II of *Paradise Lost* that he had been forced to jettison this character altogether and to replace him with the degraded Satan who appears in the later Books.

Paradise Lost, however, is neither a novel nor a drama, and Waldock's attention to speeches (or parts of speeches) and incidents fails to do justice to Milton's creation of a poetic narrative. Although ostensibly concerned with the development of the narrative in the poem, Waldock is not above considering incidents in an entirely different order from that in which Milton has placed them, or omitting vital details of their presentation. Writing, for example, of the temptation of Adam by Eve at the end of Book IX, Waldock describes the incident entirely in terms of the speeches made by the two characters, and asks us to judge whether or not Adam should have yielded on the basis of this dialogue. He fails to point out the effect of the context in which this exchange takes place and, in particular, the **symbolism** of the description of Adam's meeting with Eve: he with a garland of flowers which fade as soon as Eve tells her news, she with a bough from the Tree of Knowledge. These details are crucial both to our evaluation of the scene and to Adam's guilt.

Similarly, although Waldock censures Milton for including authorial comments about Satan which undermine the magnificence of his early speeches, Waldock himself attempts to persuade us by imagining the reaction of the fallen angels to these speeches: Milton chose when to give us these reactions and when to withhold them. Waldock, therefore, provides a critique upon a poem which is not Milton's *Paradise Lost*, and lays charges against Milton which are quite unfair. For Waldock, Hell is not described in sufficiently concrete detail, and yet, if it had been, Milton's God would have been truly vengeful and the debate among the fallen angels in Book II would have been utterly pointless – the only possible outcome of being sent to a Hell of concrete pain could be the attempt to escape.

 QUESTION

What are the advantages and disadvantages of starting a narrative *in medias res* (in the middle)?

RESPONSES FROM BURDEN, FISH AND EMPSON

Waldock's book raised some real questions about what happens in *Paradise Lost* (whether, for example, Eve's fall is of a different order from that of Adam), and prompted two detailed defences of *Paradise Lost*: one is from Dennis Burden (*The Logical Epic*, Routledge, 1967) and the other from Stanley Fish (*Surprised by Sin*, University of California Press, 1967). Both of these studies are worthy of the attention of students of *Paradise Lost*.

Burden is particularly helpful in discriminating between those parts of the poem which derive from the Bible and those which are of Milton's own invention. As modern readers, we face real difficulties in assessing the success of *Paradise Lost*, not least because our knowledge of the Bible tends to be far less detailed than that of Milton's contemporaries, and we are therefore liable to make a mistaken assessment of Milton's originality. Furthermore, we may not only have insufficient experience with other epics to be able to recognise **anti-epic** features in the poem; but we may also need constantly to remind ourselves that this massive work is the product of human invention – it is not 'given', but came about as a result of a set of choices which Milton made. The work of both Burden and Fish has done much to help the modern reader cope with these problems.

Stanley Fish's book is a detailed investigation of the process undergone in reading *Paradise Lost* and of the ways in which the reader is tempted by the attractions of the satanic epic. The thesis of the book is substantially in accord with that of Burden, and together these two critics present a lucid case for regarding *Paradise Lost* as a carefully constructed and remarkably innovative work.

 **QUESTION**

How far would you agree that all critics are to some extent biased in their approach?

William Empson is the author of one of the most provocative books on Milton ever written. *Milton's God* (Chatto and Windus, 1961) draws not only upon Empson's own atheism, but also upon his experience of having lived and taught outside Western Europe. It raises challenging questions about Milton's portrayal of God, some of which have never satisfactorily been answered.

Empson's approach in *Milton's God* differs from that of earlier detractors of Milton, including C. S. Lewis and T. S. Eliot, in that Empson has read the poem extraordinarily carefully, in order to establish the precise grounds for his dissatisfaction. His attack is in general far more illuminating, and more entertaining, than, for example, C. S. Lewis's *Preface to Paradise Lost*, which is written in support of the poem yet adopts an unchallenging stance towards it. Indeed, Empson is able to point with justification to instances of assertions by Lewis which betray an inaccurate reading of the text. Empson says, of Lewis's view of Mammon:

> Lewis treats him as a sensualist fighting down his pangs of shame – 'Honour? Love? Everybody I meet salutes me, and there is an excellent brothel round the corner.' But Milton tells us that one of the chief pains of Hell, as in human prisons, was deprivation of sex, if it may be so called (*Milton's God*, p. 53).

QUESTION

Here Empson **parodies** Lewis's description of Mammon. What are the advantages and disadvantages of using parody as a critical device?

This may look like an example of pettiness, scoring niggling points against the minor inaccuracies of one's opponent, but Empson's desire for precision of thinking in relation to *Paradise Lost* serves to indicate the fine distinctions being drawn within the poem. Occasionally Empson breaks his own rules and implies that a statement has been made in the poem when it is, in fact, Empson's own invention. Writing, for example, of the account by Beëlzebub of the creation of man, he observes: 'God sounds particularly like Zeus in this devil's account, whereas Raphael reports him later in the poem as saying he is going to create us to spite the devils' (p. 56). Raphael's account, of course, makes no mention of spite as a motive on God's part.

In general, however, Empson's thesis is rigorously and logically expounded: if God had foreknowledge, and he knew that mankind would fall even before the revolt of Satan, then the whole poem presents God in a very bad light, playing a malicious joke at the expense of his creations. The following quotation, for example, demonstrates Empson's interpretation of the raising of the Son (Christ) by God above the other angels, referred to by Empson as the 'Exaltation':

> If the Son had inherently held this position from before the
> creation of all angels, why has it been officially withheld from
> him till this day, and still more, why have the angels not
> previously been told that he was the agent of their creation? …
> to give no reason at all for the Exaltation makes it appear a
> challenge, intended to outrage a growing intellectual
> dissatisfaction among the angels with the claims
> of God (p. 102).

Empson presents serious challenges to the heart of the poem, which
have provoked a variety of answers. It is possible, for example, to
claim that Milton's purpose was to justify God's ways, and not the
existence of God himself, and that, lacking any faith in God,
Empson follows the fallen characters in the poem and is not
prepared to believe in the notion that it is possible to be obedient
without being promised some evident reward.

CRITICS ON PREDESTINATION

A number of critics have attempted to defend Milton's God on the
grounds that (unlike, for example, the God of the Calvinist
tradition) God in *Paradise Lost* does not predestine the fall of man,
nor does he deny grace to anyone. Milton's God shows neither
arbitrary pity nor favouritism, and the poem does not, therefore,
include the notion of an 'elect' whose salvation is predetermined by
God. God's speech in Book III emphasises that man is responsible
for his own fate (120–5) and that, after the fall, salvation is equally
dependent upon individual choice and action (191–3).

Milton's prose and poetry continually asserted the need for faith to
be explicit, and his statements on salvation in *De Doctrina
Christiana*, his principal theological treatise, reinforce the
impression of his commitment to a belief in the need for good
works as part of the process of salvation. Christopher Hill, in
Milton and the English Revolution (Faber, 1977) cites this passage
from *De Doctrina Christiana* as evidence of Milton's position: 'A
true and living faith cannot exist without works … Those who
persevere, not those who are elect, are said to attain salvation'
(p. 276). *Paradise Lost* also treats salvation in this fashion, although
the issue is somewhat obscured by Milton's use of the word 'elect'.

CONTEXT

The Calvinist
doctrine of
unconditional
election argues
that it is God's
mercy alone which
determines who
will be saved and
who will not:
salvation is not
dependent on
virtue, good works
or faith. Calvin
(1509–64) was a
leading figure in
the French
Protestant
movement.

In *De Doctrina Christiana* he defines the elect as those who believe and continue in the faith, and it is used in this sense in most of the instances in which it occurs in *Paradise Lost*. Thus, for example, the angels who remain loyal to God are described as elect:

> Thus while God spake, ambrosial fragrance filled
> All Heaven, and in the blessed spirits elect
> Sense of new joy ineffable diffused. (Book III: 135–8)

Milton is careful to present this group of angels as having achieved election by exercising their own free choice in deciding to remain faithful. This usage of 'elect', therefore, corresponds exactly to that of *De Doctrina Christiana*, implying the act of choosing rather than the passive state of being chosen. The difficulty is that Milton also uses the word in its more usual sense twice in *Paradise Lost*. In the final book Michael describes to Adam the flight of the Israelites from Egypt:

> the race elect
> Safe towards Canaan from the shore advance
> Through the wild desert (Book XII: 214–16)

And in Book III, in the midst of his declaration of the doctrine of salvation, Milton's God creates an exception to his own rule: 'Some I have chosen of peculiar grace / Elect above the rest; so is my will' (183–4). This latter passage seems to refer to those individuals who, like Milton himself, had been singled out by God to enact some special role in the divine scheme. Milton continued to believe in his own personal election, as he had once believed in the special favour which God extended to his chosen English nation; but this did not absolve him, and others similarly elected by God, from the obligation to do good works on Earth. Indeed, since God's chosen nation had decided not to carry through the Revolution to its full course, the obligation for Milton to remain personally firm was all the stronger.

Milton continually contrives his poem in a way which suggests that, although God may know of the outcome of Satan's temptation, the details of the process are left obscured. Thus, for example, in Book III God talks of the future fall of man, but he does not discriminate between the separate falls of Eve and Adam, nor indicate the precise

 CHECK THE BOOK

John Bunyan's *Grace Abounding to the Chief of Sinners* (1666) is an autobiographical account of the struggle between God and Satan for the writer's soul, and therefore gives an interesting insight into the theological views of a writer who is one of Milton's contemporaries.

QUESTION

What aspect of
Paradise Lost do
you find most
appealing – the
characters, the
drama or the issues
and debates raised
by the poem?

means by which Satan will bring about this fall. It seems as if the outcome of events is foreseen by God, but the motives and arguments which lead to these events are not predetermined. In a work which operates to such a large extent through debates, this means that a considerable part of the most interesting intellectual activity within *Paradise Lost* is made to seem to take place outside God's prediction. In *Milton's God*, Empson observed that:

> Milton regularly presents a fall as due to an intellectually
> interesting temptation, such that a cool judge may feel actual
> doubt whether the fall was not the best thing to do in the
> circumstances (p. 36).

These 'intellectually interesting' temptations are inventions on Milton's part, which are made to seem quite independent of God's predestined plan. They are a product of the self-awareness and freedom that Milton (and, by implication, Milton's God) gives to his characters, and which, if abused, leads not to a liberation from God but to a new kind of self-enslavement. What God says of man in Book III – 'I formed them free, and free they must remain, / Till they enthrall themselves' (124–5) – anticipates in terms of the narrative (although in biblical terms it succeeds it) the speech in Book VI of Abdiel to Satan, one of the most significant definitions in the poem:

> This is servitude,
> To serve the unwise, or him who hath rebelled
> Against his worthier, as thine now serve thee,
> Thy self not free, but to thy self enthralled. (178–81)

Paradise Lost offers a choice between, on the one hand, the true freedom of obedience to God and faith in God's providence, and, on the other hand, a life without God, which gives the illusion of freedom but is, in fact, the servitude of self-enslavement. One of the consequences of the fall is that a new distinction has to be made between 'liberty' and 'licence', the very distinction which was so significant in the debates during the English Revolution. 'Liberty', for Milton, involves obedience to God and conformity to God's ordered scheme; 'licentious' behaviour is the signal of the attempt to live outside this divine scheme, and leads ultimately to anarchy.

Milton's principal difficulty in working this discrimination between licence and liberty into the fabric of *Paradise Lost* is that his definition of liberty is static and therefore potentially less interesting than conventional notions of freedom. Adam, at the close of the poem, says that he has learned:

> that to obey is best,
> And love with fear the only God, to walk
> As in his presence, ever to observe
> His providence, and on him sole depend. (Book XII: 561–4)

But it is difficult to place such a definition of liberty at the centre of an **epic** poem and still maintain the interest of the reader. A great many critics have raised their particular version of this problem, which is a variant of the charge that Satan is too attractive to fail. Molly Mahood, taking Milton's later poem, *Paradise Regained* (1671), into her consideration, argues that 'there is little to show how "Heav'nly love shal outdoo Hellish hate" [*Paradise Lost*, Book III: 298], small demonstration of that "unexampl'd love" which compels the Son to suffer such an ordeal' (in A. Rudrum, ed., *Milton*, Macmillan, 1970, p. 245). G. A. Wilkes (*English Renaissance Studies*, Oxford University Press, 1980, pp. 272–4) holds that:

> The loss of paradise is powerfully brought home to us; the process of redemption and restoration may seem by contrast a mechanical victory ... Certainly the new Eden promised is to be superior to the Eden that has been lost ... But the realization of this is paradise outside the scheme of the poem.

Dennis Burden (*The Logical Epic*, p. 180) is driven to defend the overall scheme of the poem in this way:

> The climax of Book XII, the Incarnation, is not reached with any notable growth or development. The promises about the Messiah are not disposed in any significant order, nor do the types of Christ get bigger and better types ... Like the account of the war in Heaven in Book VI, Book XII offers for the most part less logical challenge and opportunity, and the lacklustre response which is all that it arouses in most of its readers shows how important are the logic and tautness of the poem elsewhere.

CHECK THE POEM
Milton became disillusioned with the Presbyterians (see **John Milton's life and works**) in the 1640s, partly because they were scathing about his writings on divorce, but also because they failed to allow religious toleration. In his poem 'On the New Forcers of Conscience under the Long Parliament' (1646) he wrote that 'New Presbyter is but Old Priest writ Large'.

CRITICS ON PREDESTINATION continued

However, it could be argued that this sense of disappointment, experienced by many readers of the poem, is deliberately contrived by Milton. It is consistent with the reversal of expectation endured by characters within the poem, and is part of a reworking of **epic** convention which is so radical (see **Literary background: The epic tradition**) that further development of the genre after Milton became impossible.

CONTEMPORARY APPROACHES

The practice of literary criticism underwent a significant transformation in the final quarter of the twentieth century. Put simply, there were two distinct movements. The first was a challenge to the idea that the syllabus of English Literature is fixed, and that certain texts should be required reading, and have the status of 'classics'. The second saw a growing argument that all texts, whatever their provenance, inevitably carry some bias, whether from politics, social class, gender or race, and that all readings of texts will carry similar bias on the part of the readers.

Milton criticism has been affected by these movements, and a good synopsis of the movement of critical practice in respect of the study of Milton is provided by Annabel Patterson in her introduction to *John Milton* (Longman, 1992), a collection of essays edited by her.

CHALLENGING THE CANON

Terry Eagleton, a leading figure in recent debates over literature, and himself a Marxist critic, makes the following observation on the nature of the English Studies syllabus in his influential and very readable book *Literary Theory: An Introduction* (Blackwell, 1983):

> Nobody is likely to be dismissed from an academic job for trying on a little semiotic analysis of Edmund Spenser; they are likely to be shown the door … if they question whether the 'tradition' from Spenser to Shakespeare and Milton is the best or only way to carve up discourse into a syllabus. (p. 214)

In other words, it is one thing to try new techniques (such as **semiotics**) on an 'established' writer (such as Milton's famous

QUESTION

In your view, what features of a piece of writing make it a 'classic'? Do you find this a useful concept to bear in mind when selecting texts to read or study?

predecessor Spenser), but it is quite another to question whether any writer actually is 'established' or not – whether or not he or she has produced works which are regarded as part of the canon of established literary texts.

BIAS AND IDEOLOGY

Terry Eagleton goes on to exemplify the way in which bias and ideology operate in literary criticism. For Eagleton, no reading of a text can be politically or ideologically neutral. This is borne out by what we have seen already with respect to criticism of Milton's language. F. R. Leavis was noticing something about Milton's use of language (not necessarily noticing it accurately) but failing to relate that to a wider set of his own assumptions, not least Leavis's own particular prejudices. Similarly, it is not surprising that Empson, an atheist, should find Milton's God unpalatable.

It has always been possible for readers to be prejudiced against Milton's writings because of what they believed about Milton the man: his politics, or his views on marriage, or what they had heard about his relationship with his daughters. The influence of Robert Graves's novel *Wife to Mr Milton* (1942) may account for some of these views.

It ought to be the case that evaluation of the quality of a work should operate separately from any evaluation of its writer, but all too often the two become confused. In fact, it would seem that Milton himself did not separate the writer from the writing – see the extract from his *An Apology for Smectymnuus* reproduced in **Part Five** of these Notes; but much recent criticism has attempted to do just that (see also **Literature and history** below).

FEMINISM

One particularly influential form of literary criticism in the twentieth and twenty-first centuries has been **feminism**. This form of criticism is not confined to discussion of texts by women (nor is it the sole province of women critics), but considers the treatment of gender, and of male and female viewpoints, in all texts. Not surprisingly, a great deal of the feminist criticism of *Paradise Lost* is

 CHECK THE BOOK

Robert Graves's novel *Wife to Mr Milton* (Cassell, 1942) presents Milton as being cruel and unreasonable to his first wife, Mary Powell, and the narrative is told from her point of view. It suggests that Milton married Mary simply for financial reasons. The novel enjoyed considerable popularity, and was therefore very influential in shaping the view of Milton the man.

concerned with Milton's presentation of Eve – see, for example, Diane Kelsey McColley's *Milton's Eve* (University of Illinois Press, 1983). However, readers of Books I and II might well wish to reflect upon the way in which Sin is presented in the second Book: is it fair to describe Sin, an abstraction, as a female, or would it be reasonable to regard her as an abused woman? One might also consider the significance of Milton's description of Solomon, in Book I as 'that uxorious king' (444). For further reading in this area, two good books containing feminist readings of Milton are Catherine Belsey's *John Milton: Language, Gender and Power* (Blackwell, 1988) and *Milton and the Idea of Woman*, ed. M. Walker (University of Illinois Press, 1988).

C. G. Martin (ed.), *Milton and Gender* (Cambridge University Press, 2004) contains thirteen essays from a range of critics, several of which concentrate on *Paradise Lost*. The introduction to this collection gives a helpful overview of what Milton actually wrote on the subject of women, and discriminates between the reality of his writings and the reputation they have acquired. The individual essays that follow deal in detail with specific Milton works, and the illustrations are significant too, in that they are drawn from Jane Giraud's *Flowers of Milton* (1846). Giraud was the first woman to illustrate Milton's work (and possibly the first ecofeminist critic of *Paradise Lost*).

POST-COLONIALISM

QUESTION

What elements of *Paradise Lost* Books I and II do you think lend themselves to post-colonial analysis? For example, is Satan oppressed, or an oppressor? What references to 'empire' can you find?

Another movement in twentieth-century criticism reflected in the study of Milton is **post-colonialism**. This movement is not simply confined to the study of works produced in countries formerly colonised by European powers, but also considers the presentation of colonialism and imperialism in earlier texts. For example, Emily C. Bartels, in *Spectacles of Strangeness* (University of Pennsylvania Press, 1993), looks at Christopher Marlowe's plays as post-colonial products, and considers the ways in which voyages and encounters with people of other cultures are represented. Bartels places Marlowe's plays in the context of this period of colonisation and exploration, and suggests that this context has a bearing on how non-British characters in the plays might have been received by a British audience. There are been parallel studies of the context of colonialism for Shakespeare's play *The Tempest* (1610) such as *The Tempest: A Case Study in Critical Controversy* edited by Gerald Graff and James Phelan (Macmillan, 2000).

J. M. Evans, in *Milton's Imperial Epic* (Cornell University Press, 1996), considers *Paradise Lost* as a text shaped by notions of colonial expansion, especially in North America. He suggests that:

> the poem as a whole reenacts . . . many of the central events that took place during the conquest of the New World: the voyage of discovery, the initial encounter with naked innocents . . . the establishment of the colony, the search for gold, the cultivation of the land, the conversion of the natives, the dispossession of the indigenous population, the triumphant return home. (p. 5)

The collection of essays *Milton and the imperial vision*, edited by B. Rajan and E. Sauer (Duquesne University Press, 1999) includes sixteen essays that explore Milton's work against the backdrop of imperialism and colonialism in the seventeenth century, and also extend their attention to the present-day concern with postcolonialism and postcolonialist discourse.

LITERATURE AND HISTORY

John Carey, reviewing Anna Beer's biography of Milton, *Milton: Poet, Pamphleteer and Patriot* (Bloomsbury, 2008), wrote:

> Milton's poetry gets little coverage. This is in line with current trends. Modern Milton scholars are more inclined to write about his politics than his poetry . . . Like other contemporary Miltonists, Beer regards *Paradise Lost* as a 'political allegory' of Milton's own times.

Carey clearly feels that too much attention is now being paid to Milton's politics and not enough to his poetry. He is correct in identifying an increasing trend for critics to write about Milton as an historical figure rather than to investigate the ways in which his poetry operates. This trend began in earnest with Christopher Hill's *Milton and the English Revolution* (Faber, 1976), and more recent studies by Christopher Kendrick, *Milton: A Study in Ideology and Form* (Methuen, 1986), and Laura L. Knoppers, *Historicizing Milton: Spectacle, Power and Poetry in Restoration England*

 **CHECK THE NET**

Carey's review, from *The Sunday Times*, is available online, at **www. entertainment. timesonline.co.uk** and is well worth a read. Peter Ackroyd reviews the same biography on the same site. Search Times Online for 'Anna Beer' to find both reviews.

QUESTION

Do you agree with
John Carey's
comment, that
more attention is
paid to Milton's
politics than his
poetry?

(University of Georgia Press, 1994), promote Milton as a polemicist rather than as a poet.

PREDESTINATION AND MILTON

The critical interest in predestination and free will shows no sign of abating. Harold Skulsky revisits this area of concern in *Milton and the Death of Man: Humanism on Trial in Paradise Lost* (University of Delaware Press, 2000), whilst Victoria Silver's *Imperfect Sense: the Predicament of Milton's Irony* (Princeton University Press, 2001) goes back to the arguments between William Empson and Stanley Fish.

Books by David Danielson (*Milton's Good God*, Cambridge University Press, 1982) and Neil Forsyth (*The Satanic Epic*, Princeton University Press, 2003) continue the debate over the presentation of Satan and of God: neither of these topics can ever exclude the other.

PART FIVE

BACKGROUND

HISTORICAL BACKGROUND

John Milton lived through one of the most turbulent periods of British history, a time which included the trial and execution of a monarch, and the ruling of the country by someone with no claim to the throne: these are both unique events. When Milton was born, in 1608, James I had been on the throne of England for five years. After the death of Elizabeth I, James, as the first monarch of the House of Stuart, united the thrones of England and Scotland, but he proved to be very unpopular with Parliament and with many of his people.

Believing that he had been called to rule by God's command rather than by the will of the people or the consent of their representatives, James clashed frequently and violently with Parliament over the control of the country's government, and particularly its finances. King James also thought that he should control the Church through its bishops; but a group of people, increasing in numbers and strength as the years went by, objected to the power of those bishops and to corruption in the established Church. These men, the Puritans, realised that abuses (such as one priest holding more than one living) were being retained, and resented the fact that the authority of the Pope had been replaced by that of the king as head of the English Church. The Puritans strove for a purer and more austere form of worship and Church organisation. Thus the two forces of Puritanism and Parliamentarianism together resisted the absolutism of the monarchy, at first by constitutional means, seeking reform of abuses, and then, from 1642 onwards, by force of arms.

The son of James I, Charles I, quarrelled bitterly with Parliament, from his accession in 1625 until 1629, when he tried to rule without a Parliament at all. This was neither illegal nor unconstitutional, because the king had every right to call Parliament as it suited him. A Scots invasion forced Charles to recall Parliament in 1640 to vote

CHECK THE BOOK

For further background on this period, two useful guides are *The Debate on the English Revolution* (Manchester University Press, 1998) by R. C. Richardson, and *The English Civil War: A People's History* (Harper Perennial, 2007) by Diane Purkiss.

CONTEXT

It is usual now for critics and historians to discriminate between the English Civil War and the English Revolution: the former term is used for the military campaigns of the 1640s, and the latter to the wider religious, economic and social upheavals over a much longer period.

for funds for an army, but he disagreed with them once again, only to find his chief minister, the Earl of Strafford, and his Archbishop of Canterbury, William Laud, removed from office and executed. Finally, in 1642, the king took up arms to crush the forces of Parliament in civil war.

Although successful in the early stages of the war, Charles faced a powerful combination in the alliance of Parliament with the Scots, the loyalty of London to the parliamentary cause, and the brilliant military leadership of Oliver Cromwell. As Charles's fortunes declined, he was beaten in decisive battles at Marston Moor in 1644 and Naseby in 1645. He surrendered, and was imprisoned, tried, condemned and beheaded in 1649. Thereafter Cromwell ruled as Lord Protector until his death in 1658, a period known as the Protectorate. The Commonwealth became increasingly unpopular, however, and there was no strong character to succeed Cromwell. So, in 1660, the royal House of Stuart was restored to the country's throne in the person of Charles II (Charles I's son), a man of questionable morals but of considerable political astuteness. When John Milton died in 1674, Charles II had been on the throne for fourteen years. A further fourteen years were to pass before a second revolution, this time relatively bloodless, continued the process of securing parliamentary control in the country and fashioning a constitutional monarchy.

John Milton's life and works

John Milton, born in London in 1608, believed himself to be a divinely inspired writer. From his youth onwards he considered himself capable of employing that gift in a magnificent and celebratory work. Although the **epic** which he eventually wrote declares itself to be concerned with the disobedience, and hence the folly, of mankind, it also predicts the restoration of mankind through Christ's sacrifice, and can thus claim to incorporate a subject which is both tragic and majestic.

No other English poets have been as closely involved in the political events of their time as Milton was. He was a national figure, not only supporting the Republican cause of Oliver Cromwell, but also working for Cromwell during the period of the Protectorate (see **Historical background**). Ironically, the man who has the best claim to be regarded as England's finest poet was better known to his contemporaries for his prose pamphlets than for his poems. Moreover, because of the controversial opinions which he expressed in those pamphlets, Milton was the subject of scathing comments from a number of other writers.

In consequence, we know a great deal about what Milton's contemporaries thought of him and, because Milton was ready to defend himself from attack, we have a considerable body of writing in which Milton describes himself, his life and his aspirations. For example, his 1654 pamphlet *The Second Defence of the People of England*, originally written and published in Latin, is, in large part, a defence of himself in answer to a detractor. Milton gives us in that pamphlet this account of his early life (cited from *Milton's Prose Writings*, ed. K. M. Burton, Everyman, 1974):

> My father destined me from a child to the pursuits of literature; and my appetite for knowledge was so voracious, that, from twelve years of age, I hardly ever left my studies, or went to bed before midnight. This primarily led to my loss of sight. My eyes were naturally weak, and I was subject to frequent headaches; which, however, could not chill the ardour of my curiosity or retard the progress of my improvement. My father had me daily instructed in the grammar-school, and by other masters at home. He then, after I had acquired a proficiency in various languages, and had made a considerable progress in philosophy, sent me to the University of Cambridge. Here I passed seven years in the usual course of instruction and study, with the approbation of the good, and without any stain upon my character, till I took the degree of Master of Arts.
>
> After this I did not, as this miscreant feigns, run away into Italy, but of my own accord retired to my father's house, whither I was accompanied by the regrets of most of the fellows of the college, who showed me no common marks of friendship and esteem. On my father's estate, where he had determined to pass the remainder of his days, I enjoyed an interval of uninterrupted

CHECK THE BOOK
Milton's own attitude to Cromwell is discussed by Laura Lunger Knoppers's chapter 'Late Political Prose' in *A Companion to Milton* (edited by Thomas N. Corns).

CHECK THE NET
The latest biography of Milton, by Anna Beer, was published in 2008, to coincide with Milton's quartercentenary. See **Contemporary approaches: Literature and history** for online reviews of this work. There is also a dedicated website containing resources related to the anniversary at **http://milton-2008.lib.cam.ac.uk**

CHECK THE NET
There are several portraits and engravings of Milton which indicate that he was a handsome man, including one done when he was sixty two years old. A selection of portraits is available through the links from **www.selfknowledge.com**, and the portrait of Milton at sixty-two can be accessed via the site **www.birmingham.gov.uk**

CHECK THE POEM
Milton wrote the text for a courtly entertainment (or 'Mask'), which was performed in September 1634: the music was composed by Henry Lawes. The work is commonly known as *Comus*, after its principal character.

leisure, which I entirely devoted to the perusal of the Greek and Latin classics; though I occasionally visited the metropolis, either for the sake of purchasing books, or of learning something new in mathematics or in music, in which I, at that time, found a source of pleasure and amusement. In this manner I spent five years till my mother's death. (pp. 341–2)

There is every reason to believe that this passage, although written in response to particular attacks, gives an accurate account of Milton's early life and his aspirations. He was born into a family who could afford to pay for a good quality of education for their son. He attended university, where his attractive appearance was commented upon, and where he may have quarrelled with his tutor, and certainly found the syllabus and the conversation little to his taste.

Milton's love of solitude and of self-directed study is evident in the autobiographical passage cited above, and his life was characterised by self-discipline and individualism. As far as we can gather, he made few close friends, and the one person to whom he was most attached in his youth, Charles Diodati, a school friend, died in 1638. That death and the drowning of one of Milton's fellow students, Edward King, whom Milton knew much less well than he did Diodati, caused the poet to spend time considering the brevity of life, in elegies in Latin and in English. Most notably, Milton contributed a poem in English, *Lycidas*, to a collection of poetry in memory of Edward King. Milton's early poetic output is characterised by the variety of languages he is able to employ. The greatest poet in the English language had no little facility in Italian, Latin and Greek.

After Cambridge, Milton did not train for a profession, as his brother Christopher did, nor did he enter the Church: instead, he set about pursuing his own reading at his father's estate, Horton in Buckinghamshire. He enjoyed some success as a writer during this period, producing a masque in 1634, later published under the title *Comus*.

In 1638 Milton began an extensive European tour, and it is to this event that he refers in the extract above. His detractors had claimed that Milton, aware of the increasingly difficult political situation in England, had decided to abandon his country and 'flee' to the safety of continental Europe. Milton disputes this. He cut short his tour because of the situation in England, but did not hurry unduly on his way home. Nor did he join the armies of the Parliament on his return, but devoted himself instead to the education of his two nephews, the Phillips brothers, and to the composition of pamphlets which attacked the excesses of the bishops and supported the Presbyterians.

The years 1642–3 mark the end of what might be called Milton's first period, and the beginning of his second. From a personal point of view, his prolonged education was complete. Poetically, he had already written his early lyric poems: the 'Nativity Ode'; *L'Allegro* ('the happy man') and the companion *Il Penseroso* ('the serious man'); the masque *Comus*; the pastoral elegy *Lycidas*; and a number of sonnets, among them the autobiographical 'Twenty-Third Birthday'. Moreover, his experience as a pamphleteer had taught him, even at this early stage, that his enemies would seek to discredit his ideas by attacking his own personal behaviour.

The second period of Milton's life was one of public office and political pamphleteering, with a few sonnets the only poetry he produced. After his return from his European tour, Milton had involved himself in the political controversies of the day by writing pamphlets against the bishops. In 1642 he married Mary Powell, the daughter of a Royalist household in Oxford with which his father had had business dealings; however, despite the fact that Milton obviously found Mary to be physically attractive this was primarily a marriage by arrangement, and was certainly no love match on her side.

It appears that Mary quickly found the Puritan austerity and intellectual stature of her husband too much for her, and returned home. The war made reconciliation between them difficult. Many commentators would claim that it was his own bitter personal experience which led Milton to justify divorce by reference to scripture in four pamphlets. Others point out that Milton had grounds for divorce under the existing laws, that his pamphlets, if

---

CONTEXT

The Presbyterians were the leading group within the Puritans, that group of people who wished to see the Church 'purified' of rituals which they associated with foreign religions, especially Roman Catholicism. The Puritans were more concerned with modes of worship and with the relationship between Church and State than with doctrine or theology: thus Milton attacked the bishops in his prose tracts for their avarice and corruption and for their failure to allow freedom of worship.

 CHECK THE BOOK

For more on Presbyterianism at this time, see N. H. Keble's chapter 'Milton and Puritanism' in *A Companion to Milton*.

CHECK THE BOOK

There are relatively few records of the details of Milton's personal life, so readers need to be on their guard against biographies which make extravagant claims about his marriages, especially those which draw too direct a link between his marriage to Mary Powell and his writings on divorce. A fictional account of Milton's life, Anne Manning's *Mary Powell & Deborah's Diary* (1859), is sensitive to Milton's blindness and financial difficulties in later life, and is now available in reprinted editions.

accepted, would have given women rights in the settlement of divorce much more extensive than those proposed by any of his contemporaries, and that Milton never did in fact divorce Mary: she returned to him after three years and they had four children together.

The pamphlets on divorce were condemned by Presbyterian theologians, who were already, in 1643, severely limiting the licensing of books. Milton believed that two of his most strongly held principles were endangered: the right of individual interpretation of scripture, and his freedom of speech and writing. So, in 1644, he published *Areopagitica*, his most celebrated pamphlet, inspired by love of liberty and devoid of the usual personal scurrility. His sympathies were now with Cromwell and the army section of the Parliamentarians with their greater religious tolerance, rather than with the Presbyterians. In 1649 Milton was appointed Latin Secretary to the Commonwealth with the official title of Secretary for the Foreign Tongues: the revolutionary government used Latin as its language of diplomacy, and the learned Milton was a natural choice. His main tasks were to write pamphlets justifying government policy, particularly the execution of the king; to defeat the champions of the Royalist cause on paper; and to compose official despatches to the courts of Europe, from Stockholm to Savoy. The strength of Milton's views against monarchy and against elaborate religious practices can be clearly seen in the early books of *Paradise Lost*, in which he loses no opportunity to portray kings and bishops negatively.

By 1652 Milton had lost his sight completely, and in 1655 he was allowed a substitute Secretary. He now turned his mind back to poetry, although he continued to write anti-monarchical pamphlets until 1660, the year of the Restoration.

Milton's third period was characterised by personal defeat and disillusion, but celebrated in his literary output by his three great poems *Paradise Lost*, *Paradise Regained* and *Samson Agonistes*. This final period coincided approximately with the first fourteen years of the Restoration (1660–74), though there are grounds for believing that he wrote Satan's address to the sun (*Paradise Lost*, Book IV lines 32–113) as early as 1658. At the time of the Restoration, Milton, as a well-known Cromwellian, was in some physical danger, but the Royalist poet Sir William Davenant, placing poetry before politics, concealed him until the danger had passed.

From then on, Milton – blind, ailing and impoverished – lived quietly and unpersecuted in the midst of his triumphant enemies, visited by many friends and admirers, until his death in 1674.

In the past fifty years, critics have started to pose questions of the type 'Did Milton write *Paradise Lost*?' Such a question does not imply a belief that somebody else may have written the poem (as some would seek to attribute Shakespeare's plays to Christopher Marlowe or Francis Bacon), but rather that the poem had no real 'author' at all, instead being an inevitable product of the historical moment of England after the Restoration of the monarchy. Two critics in particular have shifted attention away from the notion that there exists a single author for any text, and towards the idea that literary texts are constructed by society as a whole: the philosophers Roland Barthes and Michel Foucault produced influential essays on this matter, respectively, 'The Death of the Author' (1968) and 'What is an Author?' (1969). At this point the boundaries between literary criticism and philosophy become blurred. For further reading in this area, see the entry on 'Author' in Martin Gray's *A Dictionary of Literary Terms* (York Handbooks, Longman, 1992).

Influential among those writers who have examined the relationship between Milton's work and his contemporary situation has been the historian Christopher Hill, whose book *Milton and the English Revolution* (Faber, 1977) charts in detail the references in *Paradise Lost* to the politics of the seventeenth century. Following in Hill's line, Christopher Kendrick pursues a similar investigation in *Milton: A Study in Ideology and Form* (Methuen, 1986) while Laura L. Knoppers, in *Historicizing Milton: Spectacle, Power and Poetry in Restoration England* (University of Georgia Press, 1994), makes a convincing case that the use and frequency of such words as 'restore' and 'joy' in *Paradise Lost* are specific references to the public celebrations which followed the Restoration of Charles II.

CONTEXT

William Davenant (1606–68) was a poet and playwright. He was also rumoured to have been the illegitimate son of Shakespeare. He is sometimes credited with having introduced the word 'opera' into the English language.

CONTEXT

There is no clear evidence of what caused Milton's blindness, although it may well have been aggravated by Milton's punishing schedule of study and reading. Perhaps it is more significant to consider the effect that Milton's blindness had upon his writing and upon his life.

LITERARY BACKGROUND

The autobiographical references in Milton's prose, his letters, his Commonplace Book (his private journal), and the **allusions** to other writers throughout his work give an indication of the range of reading which he undertook in his commitment to becoming a poet. We shall never have a complete list of Milton's reading, but the selection we know of makes the study of his writing, the poetry in particular, a daunting task and scarcely a year goes by without a new source being discovered for one of his works.

From a modern perspective Milton can appear something of a conformist, a reactionary writer. He invented no new poetic forms and, even in his prose, where it might be assumed that there was scope for formal innovation, he adopted traditional **rhetorical** modes whenever possible (see **Language and style: Rhetoric**). However, we should bear in mind not only the particular political circumstances which led Milton to present himself as a respectable, establishment figure writing within an accepted tradition, but also the fact that Milton left none of these traditional modes untouched by his own originality. The **epic**, the tragedy, the masque, the pastoral elegy and the sonnet were all shaped by Milton to fresh ends, and concepts such as heroism, victory and defeat were redefined.

 QUESTION

In what ways might our knowledge of Milton as a public figure be a help in the study of his poetry, and in what ways a hindrance?

For Milton, traditions were there to be used, rather than to prescribe behaviour. He undertook rigorous personal preparation in becoming a writer, having found the syllabus at Cambridge deficient for his needs. After preparing himself for a life as a priest, he found that the practices of the conventional Church were abhorrent to him and thus devoted himself to training as a poet, only to find that events forced him to join the pamphleteering war. However, Milton saw no grave inconsistency between priesthood, poetry and prose writing. There was little fundamental distinction for him between prose and poetry, and indeed some passages from his prose read with the fervour and inspiration of poetry:

> Then, amidst the hymns and hallelujahs of saints, some one may perhaps be heard offering at high strains in new and lofty

measure to sing and celebrate thy divine mercies and marvellous judgement in this land throughout all ages.

In the passage above, from *Of Reformation* (1641), Milton is writing of the development of England as a nation and of his role as poet in celebrating that triumphal movement towards reformation. In his early Latin poem to his father, 'Ad Patrem', Milton catalogues the attributes and magnificences of poetry. Poetry was, for Milton, not only part of the educational curriculum for the cultured man, it was also a product of that education. Thus poetry did not represent a retreat from the issues of the world into pretty fancies, but an engagement with them and an attempt to mould minds and opinions through the power of words.

In *The Reason of Church Government* (1641) Milton sets out his views on the roles of poet and priest, and on the differences between good and bad poets. He says, of the gifts of poetry:

> These abilities … are the inspired gift of God, rarely bestowed, but yet to some (though most abuse) in every nation; and are of power, beside the office of a pulpit, to inbreed and cherish in a great people the seeds of virtue and public civility, to allay the perturbations of the mind, and set the affections in right tune … to deplore the general relapses of kingdoms and states from justice and God's true worship.

The poet, therefore, ranks equally with the priest as an instructor. Milton seems to feel rather as his near-contemporary George Herbert (1593–1633) does in 'The Church Porch': 'A verse may find him, / who a sermon flies, / And turn delight into a sacrifice.'

Good poetry is to be distinguished from bad poetry not on the grounds of technical deficiency (although it may be distinct in that respect too), but on the grounds of its moral content, as Milton explains in *The Reason of Church Government*:

> the writings of libidinous and ignorant poetasters; who, having scarce ever heard of that which is the main consistence of a true poem … do for the most part lay up vicious principles in sweet pills to be swallowed down, and make the taste of virtuous documents harsh and sour.

CONTEXT

The 'Reformation' was the term used in England from the sixteenth century onwards for the move away from the Roman Catholic Church towards Protestantism. It was specifically employed by those who wished to assert the affinity of the Church of England with other Protestant churches in continental Europe, including the Calvinists and the Lutheran Churches.

? **QUESTION**

QUESTION

How relevant do you find the connection between morality and literature in the twenty-first century?

CONTEXT

Marvell (1621–78), Herbert (1593–1633) and Donne (1572–1631) were poets who were active during the seventeenth century, and whose poetic style was similar enough for the eighteenth-century Samuel Johnson in his *Lives of the Most Eminent English Poets* (1779–81) (which included a biography of Milton) to label them as a group the 'metaphysical poets'. In fact they did not conceive of themselves of being a group and were hardly aware of one another.

This view is evident in Milton's earliest poetry. In *Lycidas* the virtuous and worthy characters are associated with the music of true, moral poetry: 'Who would not sing for Lycidas? He knew / Himself to sing, and build the lofty rhyme' (10–11); and harmony is equally associated with virtue in *Comus*, *L'Allegro* and *Il Penseroso*. As Milton explains in *An Apology for Smectymnuus* (1642):

> he who would not be frustrate of his hope to write well hereafter in laudable things, ought himself to be a true poem; that is, a composition and pattern of the best and honourablest things; not presuming to sing high praises of heroic men, or famous cities, unless he have in himself the experience and practice of all that is praiseworthy.

Throughout his career, Milton is careful to present himself as a 'true poem', a virtuous man whose views are therefore worth listening to, and to attack the views of his opponents because they are not 'true poems'. For Milton, the validity of an argument depended upon the integrity of the person who advanced it, and to teach this lesson was one of the functions of poetry. In this respect he was following in the direct line of writers such as Philip Sidney (1554–86) and Edmund Spenser (?1552–99), both of whom emphasised that the educational aspect of poetry was more important than its power to entertain. Milton was a great admirer of Spenser, whom he mentions in *Areopagitica* (1644) as 'our sage and serious poet'. Indeed, Milton's first volume of collected verse, *Poems 1645*, was advertised as an imitation of Spenser.

Spenser's declared aim, as stated in the preface to his epic *The Faerie Queene*, seems close to that of Milton: 'The generall end therefore of all the books is to fashion a gentleman or noble person in vertuous and gentle discipline.' Spenser, however, was able to do this without risking giving offence to those in power, because the time at which he lived, in the reign of Elizabeth, was more settled, and Spenser himself was very much an establishment figure; Milton, as a supporter of the anti-monarchists, had to take much greater risks to convey his educational message, especially after the Restoration of the monarchy in 1660.

Milton did not have to follow in the line of Sidney and Spenser. He could have done as George Herbert did before him and Andrew Marvell was to do after him; he could have written in the metaphysical style of John Donne. This witty, detached manner of writing was available for the expression of personal, political or religious ideas, but Milton chose not to adopt it.

Raymond Williams, a leading proponent of cultural theory, has characterised the difference between Milton's position and that of the metaphysical poets. Milton, he suggests, temporarily suspended what is usually called literature, but did not suspend his writing, during a brief period of conflict. The metaphysical poets, by contrast, found 'a way of holding divergent attitudes towards struggle or towards experience together in the mind at the same time' (cited by B. Sharratt, 'The Appropriation of Milton', *Essays and Studies* XXXV, 1982, p. 30). What Williams means is that Milton chose to engage with the conflict of the time by writing in a genre (the pamphlet) which was not usually regarded as a literary mode: hence Milton 'temporarily suspended what is usually called literature'.

By the time the political crisis was at its height, Donne and Herbert were dead; but in any case, the poems which they wrote describing their crisis of faith were very different both in character and in function from Milton's religious poems. They were private expressions of their individual relationships with their God, sometimes uncertain, often passionate. They are striking and dramatic and, in the case of Herbert, often deceptively simple. In neither case was Donne or Herbert writing for a public platform and, indeed, neither found a publisher for his religious verse in his own lifetime.

Milton, on the other hand, felt that the situation of the moment demanded either celebration or explanation, and was far less concerned with his own relationship with God than with the larger issues of determining what God's will for God's people might be. It is ironic that Milton should be associated in the popular mind with egoism, when there is far less self-interest in his poetry than in that of many of his contemporaries.

> **CONTEXT**
>
> In terms of the study of literature and other art forms, cultural theory and cultural studies investigate and interrogate the equation between 'culture' and 'civilisation', and the tendency to regard 'culture' as being synonymous with 'high culture': thus, by this definition, the novels of Jane Austen qualify as culture, whereas those of Dan Brown or Stephen King do not. Williams (1921–88), and those who followed after him, investigated such activities as attendance at football matches, and argued that these activities had as much claim to be viewed as culture as did attendance at opera or ballet.

Some of Milton's characters may express doubts (Satan, in particular) about the ways of God, and there may be shifts, and even inconsistencies, in Milton's views from work to work, but each individual poem or prose pamphlet attempts to convince its readers of Milton's own absolute certainty on theological issues.

When in 1649, for example, the point at issue is whether a king has a relationship with God different from that of his subjects, Milton delivers his opinion confidently: 'all men naturally were born free, being the image and resemblance of God himself, and were, by privilege above all the creatures, born to command, and not to obey' (*The Tenure of Kings and Magistrates*). In this assertion, Milton is, in a sense, working from the same basis as cultural theorists: he is claiming that kingship is simply a convention adopted within certain cultures, and that the natural state of humanity is equality. In that same pamphlet he defends the principle of regicide in these words: 'It is not . . . the glory of a protestant state never to have put their king to death; it is the glory of a protestant king never to have deserved death.'

However, Milton showed on one occasion that he could, in fact, also write in the manner of Herbert if he chose; he could investigate his own faith more personally. The beautiful sonnet 'When I consider how my light is spent', which he left unpublished for over twenty years, provides an intimate insight into Milton's private uncertainties and the way in which he resolved them.

THE GOTHIC TRADITION

Milton's presentation of Satan as a wicked, dangerous but attractive character has led to the view that Satan is the origin for the heroes of the Gothic novel, that style of fiction which became popular in the late eighteenth and early nineteenth centuries. The poet William Blake remarked that Milton was 'of the Devil's party without knowing it' and it is certainly the case that the central characters of many Gothic novels are Satan in all but name.

Horace Walpole's *The Castle of Otranto* (1764) is usually credited as the first Gothic novel, and the genre is characterised by its distinctive landscapes (wild untamed nature and ruined buildings)

CHECK THE POEM

'When I consider how my light is spent' is available online from the Milton Reading Room, under *Poems* (1673) as 'Sonnet 19 (XVI)'. Milton seems to criticise God for depriving him of sight, but the sonnet ends in calmness as Milton concludes: 'They also serve who only stand and wait.' This poem is widely available in anthologies.

and the nature of its central, male characters. These men, like Milton's Satan, are wicked, energetic, but inexplicably attractive.

A whole range of fictional characters with satanic qualities can be found in novels from Charlotte Brontë's *Jane Eyre* (1847) and Emily Brontë's *Wuthering Heights* (1847) to William Faulkner's *Light in August* (1932). The influence of *Paradise Lost* is particularly notable in Mary Shelley's *Frankenstein* (1818), in which the monster reads Milton's poem and finds in it the explanation of its problem (Everyman edition, 1963):

> I often referred the several situations, as their similarity struck me to my own. Like Adam, I was apparently united by no link to any other being in existence; but his state was far different from mine in every other respect. He had come forth from the hands of God a perfect creature, happy and prosperous, guarded by the especial care of his Creator … but I was wretched, helpless, and alone. Many times I considered Satan as the fitter emblem of my condition; for often, like him, when I viewed the bliss of my protectors, the bitter gall of envy rose within me. (pp. 135–6)

In many respects Mary Shelley's novel is tantamount to a reinterpretation of *Paradise Lost*. Her attempt to translate her reading of Milton's **epic** into the medium of the Gothic novel is as revealing as the heroic opera, for which Milton gave his permission, *The State of Innocence and Fall of Man* (1678) by John Dryden (1631–1700).

Although the Gothic novel dates from the middle of the eighteenth century, the concerns with which it deals have a much older history. Gothic refers to a style of architecture from the Middle Ages, and also to a group of people, the Goths, who were part of the movement which destroyed the Holy Roman Empire. The Goths, along with the Vandals and the Huns, were, therefore, seen as explicitly anti-Christian (and specifically opposed to Roman Catholicism). The term 'vandal' is still used to denote someone bent on destroying what is valued by others, and vandals therefore represent a threat to certain notions of civilisation. Similarly, the word 'goth' is applied in contemporary culture to young people

CHECK THE BOOK

For further discussion of Milton's influence on the Romantic view of Satan, see K. Gross, 'Satan and the Romantic Satan: a notebook' in *Re-Membering Milton*, (eds) M. Nyquist and M. Ferguson (Methuen, 1987) and, for a more wide-ranging treatment of Milton and Romanticism, Leslie Brisman, *Milton's Poetry of Choice and Its Romantic Heirs* (Cornell University Press, 1973).

whose distinctive style of dress and music expresses their wish to distance themselves from the values of mainstream society. These anti-establishment connotations are part of the basis of the Gothic.

The seeds of the Gothic novel lie in those earlier literary works which show a threat to Christian values, present humans as flawed and likely to succumb to temptation, and demonstrate a preoccupation with death and superstition, without the promise of salvation or an afterlife. For example, some of the earliest examples of drama in England have the Devil presented on stage: the medieval cycles of miracle or mystery plays start with the Devil tempting Eve and end with Christ's Harrowing of Hell (although we do not know how many of the audience would have stayed until this final scene). At the outset, the Devil is wily and artful, and too potent an adversary for the innocence of Eve.

It is a short step, but a significant one, to Christopher Marlowe's *Doctor Faustus* (*c*.1592) in which the Devil's emissary, Mephistopheles, tempts the far-from-innocent Faustus to give up his soul. In Shakespeare's *Macbeth* (*c*.1603), the Devil does not appear, but there are witches and ghosts and apparitions, all of which feed into the full-blown Gothic tradition of later centuries. There is a sense in all of these earlier precursors of Gothic of despair in the face of death and a disbelief in the possibility of forgiveness or redemption. Satan suffers a similar sense of despair in *Paradise Lost* Book IV when he first sees Eden: he cannot believe that repentance and forgiveness is possible for him. In a sense, Milton re-writes *Doctor Faustus* so that it is not Faustus at the centre being tempted but Mephistopheles.

The Gothic novel, therefore, frequently centres on a hero (or a villain, and it is not always clear which is the more appropriate label) who resolutely refuses to be constrained by the conventions of society or by its Christian morality. The opening books of *Paradise Lost* centre on a hero (or villain) who goes even further by rejecting not just Christianity but rejecting his creator, God.

CHECK THE BOOK

Gothic does not draw on drama alone. Chaucer's poem *The Pardoner's Tale* (*c*.1394) is based on the notion of killing Death and succumbing to temptation: *Paradise Lost* Book II includes Death and Sin as characters whom Satan encounters as he leaves Hell.

THE EPIC TRADITION

In order to appreciate fully Milton's achievement in *Paradise Lost*, it is necessary to have an understanding of the **epic** tradition in which he casts his poem, and of the position which he believed *Paradise Lost* to occupy within that tradition.

In Book II we are introduced to an example of the composition of an epic within *Paradise Lost* itself. In the description of the way the fallen angels occupy themselves after Satan has departed we find that the fourth group of angels chooses to compose an epic:

> Sing
> With notes angelical to many a harp
> Their own heroic deeds, and hapless fall
> By doom of battle (547–50)

The fallen angels' epic seems designed to portray a false and flattering view of their history – their actions are hardly 'heroic', and their fall in battle is anything but 'hapless'. This connection between epic and history, to which Milton draws our attention, is a key to the understanding of the epic tradition.

Two writers of very different temperaments have provided similar statements on the relationship between epic and history. Samuel Johnson wrote, in *The Lives of the Most Eminent English Poets* (1783), that an epic:

> relates some great event in the most affecting manner. History must supply the writer with the rudiments of narration, which he must improve and exalt by a nobler art, animate by dramatic energy and diversify, by retrospection and anticipation.

The American poet Ezra Pound put the same idea more succinctly in 1961: 'An epic is a poem including history' (cited by P. Merchant in *The Epic*, Methuen, 1971, p. 1). The notion of this link between epic form and historical content is one which has persisted from the beginnings of the genre through to the current use of the term 'epic' in popular prose: a novel (or film) such as *Gone with the Wind* or *East of Eden* will be labelled 'epic', not merely because of its length

CONTEXT

Johnson's work was an appraisal of over fifty English poets, together with brief details of their lives. Although Johnson writes about some poets who are still highly regarded in the twenty-first century, many of the writers included in his book are now virtually unknown, and their work unread.

CONTEXT

Ezra Pound (1885–1972) was born in the USA, but spent much of his adult life in Europe. He was a poet, a critic and a founder of the Modernist movement. His involvement in politics in the 1940s led to his being tried for treason in the USA.

CHECK THE FILM

Gone with the Wind (Victor Fleming, 1939) is one of the most celebrated films of all time. It is based upon Margaret Mitchell's novel, set in the south of the USA during the American Civil War and Reconstruction.

but because it embraces a wide sweep of history and because its central characters are to be regarded somehow as representative of a particular stratum of society.

Even when the term is used of a sporting encounter – a football match which remains unresolved after two replays, or a fifteen-round heavyweight boxing contest – it is not length alone which leads to this usage, but the suggestion that this event has been memorable enough to merit a place in the folk-mythology of the town or country of which the protagonists are representative.

By tradition, epics are long narrative poems, majestic both in theme and style. They deal with legendary or historical events of national or universal significance, involving action of broad sweep and grandeur. Moreover, most epics deal with the exploits of a single representative individual, thereby giving unity to the composition. There is thus usually no confusion as to who is the hero of the epic. Often, an epic involves the introduction of supernatural forces that shape the action, conflict in the form of battles or other physical combat, and certain stylistic conventions: an invocation to the Muse, a formal statement of the theme, long lists of the protagonists involved, and set speeches couched in elevated language. All of these conventions are in evidence in *Paradise Lost*.

The poet Alexander Pope, writing a **parody** of a definition of an epic in the style of a cooking recipe, neatly summarised its essentials (cited by P. Merchant in *The Epic*, Methuen, 1971):

> Take out of any old Poem, History-books, Romances, or Legend … those Parts of Story which afford most Scope for long Descriptions … Then take a Hero, whom you may chuse for the Sound of his Name, and put him into the midst of these Adventures: There let him *work*, for twelve Books; *For the Moral and Allegory*. These you may Extract out of the Fable afterwards at your Leisure: Be sure you strain them sufficiently (p. 64).

CONTEXT

Alexander Pope (1688–1744) was a poet, essayist and a translator of classic epics. He is one of the most celebrated poets of the eighteenth century.

Throughout *Paradise Lost*, however, Milton constantly dismisses the kind of epic based upon historical adventure. Such poetry has become, for Milton, mere 'fable', a term which he tends to employ pejoratively. Milton has chosen not to follow the example of European poets like Luís de Camões (1524–80) who, in *Os Luciados*, celebrated the history of the Portuguese people. Neither does he imitate Edmund Spenser's *The Faerie Queene*, a **panegyric** for the England of Elizabeth I. Milton is employing poetry in his epic not to celebrate history but to explain it and, at times, to suggest that the interpretation of recent events by his contemporaries was flawed.

In part, however, Milton's reasons for selecting a subject for his poem which was not drawn from English history would be similar to those of Abraham Cowley, who wrote in the preface to his own epic on the life of David (1656): 'It is not without grief and indignation that I behold that *Divine Science (Poesie)* employing all her inexhaustible riches … in the wicked and beggerly *Flattery* of great persons.'

CONTEXT

Abraham Cowley (1618–67) was a poet and a supporter of the Royalist cause during the Civil War.

The traditional epic implied an association between the aspirations of the poet and that of the nation the poet was celebrating and, as in the case of *The Faerie Queene*, could hardly avoid some measure of flattery of the head of that nation. Milton could not, therefore, compose a traditional epic after the failure of his hopes for a revolution (see **Background: Milton's life and works**): the English nation of the Restoration was not a possible subject for his celebration, and thus his epic sets out to denigrate the traditional preoccupations of nationhood and individual achievement. Having described the fallen angels writing a false epic in Book II, Milton returns, towards the end of *Paradise Lost*, to question the traditional subjects of the epic (Book XI: 689–97):

> in those days might only shall be admired,
> And valour and heroic virtue called;
> To overcome in battle, and subdue
> Nations, and bring home Spoils with infinite
> Manslaughter, shall be held the highest pitch
> Of human glory …
> Destroyer rightlier called and plagues of men.

This is a radical redefinition of the central concern of traditional epics, the victory in battle of one race over another. Such battles are, in Milton's terms, manslaughter and destruction, and therefore do not constitute true heroism.

Thus Milton's **epic** differs from that of Spenser not simply because it comes later in time, and is therefore able to build upon it; nor even because Milton was a better poet than Spenser (although few would dispute that he is). It differs because the social and historical changes which had occurred between Spenser's time and that of Milton made it impossible for Milton to develop the epic within the conventional nationalistic tradition of which Spenser was a part.

Epic poems were not intended merely to be entertaining stories of legendary or historical heroes; their role was to summarise and express the nature or ideals of an entire nation at a significant or crucial period of its history; this is the function of the ancient Greek epics – the *Iliad* and the *Odyssey*, for example. Thus the characteristics of the hero of a traditional epic are likely to be national rather than individual traits, and the exercise of those traits in heroic deeds serves to gratify a sense of national pride.

The conventional epic is inherently retrospective, rehearsing the earlier triumphs of a nation in order to reassure its present citizens – just as Satan tries to rouse the fallen angels at the beginning of *Paradise Lost* by telling them stories of their 'glorious past'. Milton has therefore changed this perspective drastically by setting out to go beyond the task of merely explaining how things came to be the way they are, and suggesting instead that the history has not yet been completed, and that things may yet change. *Paradise Lost* describes the continuing failure of humanity, the blindness of the majority, and celebrates the providence of God, a providence which has yet to be totally realised.

CHECK THE BOOK

There is a good general account of the pastoral poet in *The Penguin Dictionary of Literary Terms and Literary Theory* (Penguin, 1999) by J. A. Cuddon.

By electing not to describe the triumphs of humanity up to a particular point in past history, and instead implying that there is no fixed point, the Restoration of the monarchy can be accounted for and accommodated within Milton's scheme as a purely temporary phenomenon, a further instance of the error of the majority. *Paradise Lost* implies that the error of Restoration will eventually be reversed; but that reversal, like the redemption of humanity by the Son, lies outside the scope of the history of the poem.

The decision to treat history in this manner has a direct effect on the narrative perspective. History in *Paradise Lost* is either distorted or telescoped and startling effects are produced, such as the combination of epic and pastoral conventions when Satan reaches Eden. Milton's pastoral setting is not, as it might have been conventionally, on the periphery of the poem, a place of temporary solace for a battle-weary warrior: it is the central location of the poem, and the place to which we all must aspire.

One result of this means of treating history is that it is virtually impossible to read the narrative line of *Paradise Lost* as if it had a beginning, a middle and an end, as, for example, William Empson's interpretation (see **Critical history: Responses from Burden, Fish and Empson**) would imply.

The 'partial' song of the fallen angels in Book II lines 547–50 seems, if detached from its context, the stuff of conventional epic, and Milton leaves readers at this stage of the poem to draw their own conclusions about the morality of the angels' satanic epic. It becomes clear, however, from Raphael's account of the war in Heaven much later in the poem (Books V and VI), that the battle was far from glorious, and that it was, if anything, somewhat ridiculous and pointless: in the fallen angels' epic Satan is a hero, whereas the true history shows him to have been vain and self-absorbed. One lesson to be drawn might be that Milton intended his readers to equate the satanic view of history with that of the Royalists, and to decide that the apparent victory of the Restoration would eventually be proved to have been an illusion.

Paradise Lost is a great poem, but it is also an illusive poem, and quite deliberately and consistently so. Just as Satan's invention of a glorious past is frustrated by the reality of the war in Heaven, and his ambition of victory over mankind gives way to the anticlimax of deception by an apple (an irony which even Satan finds amusing), so the reader's expectations and hopes are continually frustrated by a poem which denies glory to activity and substitutes instead the

CONTEXT

The genre of pastoral literature goes back to the poet Theocritus, writing in Greece in the fourth century BC. In brief, it presents an idealised rural world, free from the defects which the writer sees as characterising urban society (ambition, greed etc.). Pastoral poetry had become increasingly critical of contemporary urban (or courtly) life by Milton's time. However, the readers and the writers of these poems were themselves educated and urban: pastoral therefore presented an idealised version of the rural to an urban audience. Milton, in *Paradise Lost*, presents a vision of an unfallen world to a fallen readership.

primacy of obedience, an attribute which includes being obedient enough to do nothing if the need for inaction should arise. Milton is continually asserting the futility of action throughout the poem. The crisis of the world is not going to be resolved by a single, gloriously flamboyant military victory, any more than the issues of the civil war in England were settled at battles such as Naseby or Worcester. The conventional **epic**, however, reassures its readers with just that fiction: it operates through a narrative in which military heroism on the part of a minority can overcome evil for the majority, who abdicate their problems to the conventional hero. The majority will be happy to abdicate responsibility for their fate in this way, and conventional epic reinforces this willingness by rewarding its readers with stories of heroes who will fight on their behalf. *Paradise Lost* does not do this: nobody secures victory for the readers, and they are left only with the promise that Christ will one day return to win a victory for all.

THE ENGLISH EPIC

Paradise Lost is written in English, and yet one of the two commendatory poems published in the 1674 edition, that by Samuel Barrow, was written in Latin. At this point in time, English had not yet fully supplanted Latin as a language capable of being used for the most serious subjects. Milton himself wrote Latin and Greek poetry as well as poetry in English, and, in the period when he worked for Cromwell's administration (see **Background: John Milton's life and works**), his prose documents were composed in Latin too. In the Renaissance it was becoming increasingly the case that European nations were seeking to advance the status of their own vernacular languages, and one form of promoting them came through having an epic composed in that tongue.

Edmund Spenser had begun the process of securing for England its first epic in English, in his uncompleted poem *The Faerie Queene*, but Barrow recognised that Milton's achievement was greater, both in terms of its subject matter and in that it was written in this country (Spenser was writing in Ireland): 'Who that has hoped for this would believe that it would ever be written? And yet the land of Britain reads these things today' (Gordon Campbell, ed., *John*

CHECK THE BOOK
The twenty-volume edition of the *Oxford English Dictionary (OED)* is an invaluable resource for the history of the meanings of words in the English language. You will find it in most public libraries.

Milton, Complete English Poems, Of Education, Areopagitica, 1990, p. 145).

There had in fact been an epic in English even before Spenser: the Anglo-Saxon period produced the magnificent poem *Beowulf*. However, the manuscript of that early poem was undiscovered and inaccessible in Milton's time and in that era the line of English poetry tended to be traced back only as far as Geoffrey Chaucer (*c.*1343–1400).

Milton was more interested in his literary relationship with the great classical poets than in a relationship with any English writer, but the descriptions in Book II of Sin and Death and, to a lesser extent, of Chaos, demonstrate his debt to Spenser. Furthermore, alongside the many biblical and classical **allusions** (see **Detailed summaries**), there are also many references in Books I and II to Milton's own contemporary situation in England, especially in his disparaging references to kings and to churches.

QUESTION

Is there still a case to be made today for regarding poetry as the most prestigious literary medium?

Historical events	Author's life	Literary events
		1590 Edmund Spenser, *The Faerie Queene* (Books I–III)
		1596 Spenser, *The Faerie Queene* (Books IV–VI)
		1599 Death of Spenser
	1608 Born on 9 December in Bread Street, London	
		1609 William Shakespeare, *Sonnets*
		1610 Ben Jonson, *The Alchemist*
		1616 Death of Shakespeare
	1620 Attends St Paul's School around this time	
		1621 Birth of Andrew Marvell
1625 Charles I crowned King of England and Ireland	**1625** Begins study at Cambridge University	
1629 Charles dissolves Parliament	**1629** Awarded BA; writes 'Nativity Ode'	**1629** William Davenant, *The Just Italian*
		1631 Death of John Donne
	1632 Writes *L'Allegro* and *Il Penseroso*; 'On Shakespeare' published in the Second Folio edition of Shakespeare's plays	
1633 William Laud appointed Archbishop of Canterbury		**1633** Donne's *Poems* published posthumously
	1634 *Comus* performed (published 1637)	
		1637 Death of Jonson
	1638 Publication of *Lycidas;* Milton travels abroad, meeting Galileo while in Italy	

Historical events	Author's life	Literary events
1639–40 The two Bishops' Wars between Charles I and the Scottish Covenanters end in bankruptcy for Charles I and the establishment of the Long Parliament		
1640 The Long Parliament impeaches Laud; Charles I's principal adviser Strafford is executed		
	1641 Writes a number of anti-prelatical tracts	
1642 Civil War breaks out	**1642** Writes more anti-prelatical pamphlets; marries Mary Powell, who leaves him later in the year	
	1643 Publishes the first of four tracts on divorce which are met with public outcry	**1643** William Prynne, *The Sovereign Power of Parliaments*
1644 Oliver Cromwell leads Parliamentarians to victory at the battle of Marston Moor	**1644** Publishes *Areopagitica* (on freedom of speech), *Of Education* and a second tract on divorce	
1645 Laud is executed; Parliament establishes the New Model Army, which defeats Charles's forces at the battle of Naseby	**1645** Publishes two more pamphlets on divorce and *Poems 1645,* his first collection of poetry; Mary returns	
	1646 Birth of daughter Anne	
1647 Charles is arrested but escapes		**1647** Henry More, *Philosophical Poems*
1648 Charles is re-arrested	**1648** Birth of daughter Mary	
1649 Charles is executed at Whitehall	**1649** Appointed Secretary of Foreign Tongues to the Council of State; writes two tracts on Charles's execution	

Historical events	Author's life	Literary events
	1650 By now almost totally blind	**1650** Marvell, 'An Horatian Ode upon Cromwell's Return from Ireland'; Thomas Hobbes, *De Corpore Politico*
	1651 Writes his official defence of the Commonwealth; birth of son John	**1651** Davenant, *Gondibert*
	1652 Birth of daughter Deborah; death of wife Mary and son John	
1653 Cromwell establishes Protectorate		
	1654 Publishes second defence of the Commonwealth	
	1655 *Defence of Himself*	**1655** Marvell, *First Anniversary of the Government under the Lord Protector*
	1656 Marries Katherine Woodcock	
1657 Cromwell refuses the offer of the crown	**1657** Daughter Katherine born; Andrew Marvell is appointed an assistant to Milton	
1658 Death of Oliver Cromwell; his son Richard succeeds as Lord Protector	**1658** Death of wife Katherine and daughter Katherine	
1659 Richard Cromwell abdicates	**1659** Publishes two tracts on religious freedom	**1659** John Dryden, *Poem upon the Death of His Late Highness Oliver Lord Protector*

Historical events	Author's life	Literary events
1660 Restoration of the monarchy following the collapse of the Protectorate; Charles II becomes king	**1660** Writes a tract in favour of the Commonwealth; following the Restoration, Milton is imprisoned briefly and his books are publicly burned	
		1661 Dryden, *To His Sacred Majesty*
	1663 Marries Elizabeth Minshull	
1666 Great Fire of London		
	1667 Publication of *Paradise Lost* in 10 Books	**1667** Dryden, *Annus Mirabilis*
	1671 Publication of *Paradise Regained* and *Samson Agonistes*	
	1674 Second edition of *Paradise Lost,* in 12 Books; dies on 8 November	

There are hundreds of books, chapters and articles on *Paradise Lost*, and even more on Milton in general. The vast majority of these are concerned with the epic poem as a whole, not just its opening two Books. Perhaps the most obvious further reading would therefore be to become acquainted with the whole of *Paradise Lost*. Without such an acquaintance these opening Books do not make full sense.

What follows is an attempt to include a range of recent Milton criticism, together with significant works which have been referred to elsewhere in these Notes, and which are likely to be found in libraries: these include studies by William Empson, C. S. Lewis and others. For readers wishing to keep abreast of the most recent Milton scholarship, it is worth browsing through *Milton Quarterly*, reading the *Year's Work in English Studies*, or consulting the *Milton Review* website at **http://facultystaff.richmond.edu/~creamer/ review.html**. The online Milton Reading Room also has a bibliography which includes links to a range of Milton criticism, some of it accessible from the web.

In addition, the list includes selected recent works of criticism and biographical studies. Readers should be on their guard when consulting lists of books online, especially those given a publication date of 2008. This year saw the four hundredth anniversary of Milton's birth and many new books on Milton were first published then; however, several much older studies of Milton were reprinted in 2008, and readers need to know that these are not as recent as the publication dates might suggest. These include works by Mark Pattison, Richard Garnett, William Ellery Channing, Joseph Ivimey and Walter Alexander Raleigh. Although all these works represent significant landmarks in Milton criticism, they are not new books: Raleigh's is the most modern of these studies, and it was first published in 1900.

EDITIONS

J. Broadbent (ed.), *John Milton Paradise Lost Books I–II*, Cambridge University Press, 1972
  This is the edition on which these Notes are based

G. Campbell (ed.), *John Milton: Complete English Poems, Of Education, Areopagitica*, Everyman, 1980
  A good anthology of Milton's poetry and selected prose

A. Fowler (ed.), *Milton: Paradise Lost*, Longman, 1968
  A detailed edition of the epic

D. S. Kastan (ed.), *Paradise Lost*, Hacket, 2005
  This edition has a superb Introduction. It is Kastan's revision of Merilt Y. Hughes's classic 1962 edition of the poem

SELECTED GOTHIC TEXTS

Charlotte Brontë, *Jane Eyre*, 1847

Emily Brontë, *Wuthering Heights*, 1847

Geoffrey Chaucer, *The Pardoner's Tale*, c.1390

Christopher Marlowe, *Doctor Faustus*, c.1592

William Shakespeare, *Macbeth*, c.1603

Mary Shelley, *Frankenstein*, 1818

Bram Stoker, *Dracula*, 1897

Horace Walpole, *The Castle of Otranto*, 1764

CRITICAL WORKS

C. Belsey, *John Milton*, Blackwell, 1988
A feminist study referred to in Part Four of these Notes

F. Blessington, *Paradise Lost and the Classical Epic*, Routledge, 1979
Relates *Paradise Lost* to its classical antecedents

D. Burden, *The Logical Epic*, Routledge, 1967
A key study of the epic from the 1960s

D. Danielson, *Milton's Good God*, Cambridge University Press, 1982
Danielson's study is part of the critical debate on the presentation of God

T. S. Eliot, *On Poetry and Poets*, Faber, 1957
This includes an influential critique of Milton

W. Empson, *Milton's God*, Cambridge University Press, revised 1981
Empson writes of Milton's representation of God from the standpoint of an atheist

J. M. Evans, *Milton's Imperial Epic*, Cornell University Press, 1996
A post-colonial study of *Paradise Lost*

S. M. Fallon, *Milton's Peculiar Grace: Self-representation And Authority*, Cornell University Press, 2006
This is a complex text in which the author argues that Milton, because he does not write of his own sin, is not a religious writer

Further Reading

H. Fisch, *The biblical presence in Shakespeare, Milton, and Blake*, Oxford University Press, 1999
  Includes a single chapter on *Paradise Lost*

S. Fish, *Surprised by Sin*, University of California Press, 1967
  Fish considers how readers respond to *Paradise Lost*, and how Milton plays upon these responses

—, *How Milton Works*, Harvard University Press, 2001
  Fish explores the effect of Milton's theological convictions on his writing

N. Forsyth, *The Satanic Epic*, Princeton University Press, 2003
  Forsyth returns to the issue of how God and Satan are presented in *Paradise Lost*

P. C. Herman, *Destabilizing Milton: 'Paradise Lost' and the Poetics of Incertitude*, Palgrave/St Martin's Press, 2005
  Examines the lack of stability or certainty in *Paradise Lost*

C. Kendrick, *Milton: A Study in Ideology and Form*, Methuen, 1986
  This study concentrates on the historical background to Milton's poetry

J. King, *Milton and religious controversy*, Cambridge University Press, 2000
  Concerned with religious abuse, satire and polemic and how they underpin *Paradise Lost*

L. L. Knoppers, *Historicizing Milton: Spectacle, Power and Poetry in Restoration England*, University of Georgia Press, 1994
  Relates Milton's poetry to the representation of power and authority in his time

C. S. Lewis, *A Preface to Paradise Lost*, Oxford University Press, 1942
  A brief but very influential study of the poem

D. Loewenstein, *Milton: Paradise Lost (A Student Guide)*, Cambridge University Press, 2004
  Places the poem in its literary, religious, and political contexts

W. Pallister, *Between Worlds: The Rhetorical Universe of 'Paradise Lost'*, University of Toronto Press, 2008
  An analysis of Milton's rhetoric in relation to the presentation of Heaven, Hell and Paradise

C. Ricks, *Milton's Grand Style*, Oxford University Press, 1963
  A defence of Milton's language, which includes analysis of passages from *Paradise Lost*

H. Skulsky, *Milton and the death of man: humanism on trial in Paradise Lost*, University of Delaware Press, 2000
  A complex consideration of free will in *Paradise Lost*

V. Silver, *Imperfect sense: the predicament of Milton's irony*, Princeton University Press, 2001
  An analysis of the presentation of free will and predestination

SURVEYS OF HISTORICAL AND LITERARY BACKGROUND

H. Erskine-Hill and G. Storey (eds), *Revolutionary Prose*, Cambridge University Press, 1983
Includes examples of the prose of the period

B. Ford, *The New Pelican Guide to English Literature*, vol. 3, Penguin, 1980
A standard text placing the literature of the time in its historical context

C. Patrides and R. Waddington (eds), *The Age of Milton*, Manchester University Press, 1980
A very full survey of the background against which Milton wrote

MILTON'S LIFE

A. Beer, *Milton: Poet, Pamphleteer and Patriot*, Bloomsbury, 2008
A biography by a well-known scholar: its critical reception by reviewers is noted in Part Four

G. Campbell and T. N. Corns, *John Milton: Life, Work, and Thought*, Oxford University Press, 2008
This is a careful piece of work from two established and respected Milton scholars

H. Darbishire (ed.), *The Early Lives of Milton*, Constable, 1932
This work brings together the work of Milton's earliest biographers

J. Diekhoff, *Milton on Himself*, Cohen and West, 1939
A collection of all the autobiographical references in Milton's work

N. Forsyth, *John Milton: A Biography*, Lion Publishing, 2008
A scholarly work, but one which remains accessible

C. Hill, *Milton and the English Revolution*, Faber, 1977
An attempt to locate Milton in his historical context

B. K. Lewalski, *The Life of John Milton: a critical biography*, Blackwell, 2000
A biography which focuses on Milton's writing

W. R. Parker, *Milton: A Biography*, Oxford University Press, 1968
This is the yardstick for all Milton biographies of the past forty years

COLLECTIONS OF CRITICAL ESSAYS

T. Corns (ed.), *A Companion to Milton*, Wiley Blackwell, 2003
A collection of twenty-nine essays which cover a wide range of topics relevant to the study of *Paradise Lost*. This collection is referred to on a number of occasions in these Notes

A. Duran (ed.), *A Concise Companion to Milton*, Wiley Blackwell, 2006
Fourteen essays, especially useful on Milton's historical and cultural context

D. Loewenstein and P. Stevens (eds), *Early Modern Nationalism and Milton's England*, University of Toronto Press, 2008)
  Fifteen essays on the significance of the nation in Milton's work

C. G. Martin (ed.), *Milton and Gender*, Cambridge University Press, 2004
  A collection of essays considering Milton from a feminist perspective

B. Rajan and E. Sauer (eds), *Milton and the imperial vision*, Duquesne University Press, 1999
  Sixteen essays focusing on imperialism and colonialism in the seventeenth century

M. Walker (ed.), *Milton and the Idea of Woman*, University of Illinois Press, 1988
  A collection of essays on the representation of the female in Milton, some of which are concerned with *Paradise Lost*

REFERENCE

W. B. Hunter (ed.), *A Milton Encyclopaedia*, Associated University Press, 1978–80
  This has been the standard reference work on Milton for some years

INTERNET RESOURCES

In addition to books and articles published in print, students of Milton in the twenty-first century are fortunate in having access to a number of scholarly websites devoted to the poet.

At **http://www.dartmouth.edu** you will find the Milton Reading Room, which includes editions of Milton's poems and some of his prose works: these are supplied with useful footnotes.

The site at **www.literature.org** and the Project Gutenberg site at **http://www.gutenberg.org** both include a range of literary texts, including some by Milton. *Milton Review* and the Milton List can be found at **http://facultystaff.richmond.edu/~creamer/milton/index.html**

The Luminarium site at **http://www.luminarium.org** gives access to a host of resources on Milton and his contemporaries.

One of the most recent of the online Milton sites is Darkness Visible, at **http://www.christs.cam.ac.uk/darknessvisible**, which was launched in 2008 from Christ's College, Cambridge, where Milton was a student. It includes a range of resources, some of which are not found on other websites.

alliteration a sequence of repeated consonantal sounds, usually at the beginning of words or of stressed syllables

allusion a passing reference in a work of literature to something external to the work (such as another work of literature, a legend, a cultural belief or a historical fact)

anti-epic a work that employs the conventions of the traditional **epic** but subverts them, either for comic effect (for example, by having a trivial subject matter or a ridiculous hero), or, in the case of *Paradise Lost*, to suggest that all previous traditional epics are deficient

blank verse unrhymed lines of verse each containing five iambs (**iambic pentameters**). An iamb is the commonest metrical foot in English verse, consisting of an unstressed syllable followed by a stressed syllable

epic a long narrative poem in an elevated style. Typical epic themes include myth, legend, and the birth and destruction of nations – see **Literary background: The epic tradition**

epic simile a long **simile**, sometimes extended over more than twenty lines, which typically interrupts the narrative of a poem, allowing the poet to make detailed comparisons

epigram originally, an inscription on a monument. The term 'epigrammatic' is now used to describe any short poem which has a sharp turn of thought or point, be it witty, amusing or satirical

feminism a tenet of feminist thought is that male ways of perceiving and ordering are 'inscribed' into the prevailing ideology of society. In terms of literary criticism, this can be disclosed by studying language itself, and texts, in order to discover the characteristic assumptions which are inherent in them

flyting versified abuse: a quarrel in poetry between warriors about to do battle

hero in its simplest sense, the chief character in a work of literature. In relation to *Paradise Lost*, Milton uses the term to refer to a person of superhuman ability who leads, and is revered by, his people. Many earlier **epics** had been the stories of just such men, who were regarded as having saved their nations. Milton is concerned to argue that military prowess is only one form of courage, and that the heroism of the Son in *Paradise Lost* is manifest not in his military valour but in his patient and silent suffering on behalf of all humanity. See also **Critical approaches: Satan and drama**

iambic pentameter a line of poetry consisting of five iambic feet (iambic consisting of a weak syllable followed by a strong one)

imagery in its narrowest sense an image is a picture in words – a description of some visible scene or object. More commonly, however, 'imagery' refers to the figurative language in a work of literature, such as **metaphors** and **similes**; or all the words which refer to objects and qualities which appeal to the senses and feelings

in medias res (Latin: 'into the middle of things') a phrase describing a common technique of storytelling in which the **narrator** begins not at the beginning of a story or action, but in the middle, going back to recount earlier events at a later stage, or letting them emerge during the course of the story. This is a convention of the **epic**, but also occurs in the novel (for example, Emily Brontë's *Wuthering Heights*)

metaphor a departure from literal writing which goes further than a comparison (or **simile**) between two different things or ideas by fusing them together: one thing is described as being another thing

metre the rhythmic arrangement of syllables in poetic verse

narrator the person who tells the story. In many works of literature the narrator can be distinguished from the author of a work, and is the fictional person who we choose to accept as having constructed the narrative. In the case of *Paradise Lost*, however, John Milton can be regarded as both author and narrator

oxymoron a figure of speech in which contradictory terms are brought together in what seems at first to be an impossible combination, for example: 'Chained on the burning lake' (Book I: 210). An oxymoron is thus a special form of **paradox**

panegyric a public speech or poem which wholeheartedly praises someone or something

paradox a bringing together of terms which seem to contradict into a combination which has an underlying meaning, truth or humour

parody an imitation of a specific work of literature or style, devised so as to ridicule its characteristic features. In an extreme form, parody can become so grotesque and ludicrous as to be a travesty

personification a figurative use of language in which things or ideas are treated as if they were human beings, with human attributes and feelings. Examples in *Paradise Lost* include Sin, Death and Chaos: Death is described as if he could feel anger

post-colonialism the varied literatures of the many countries whose political existence has been shaped by the experience of colonialism are seen by post-colonialist critics to share basic characteristics, especially in relation to their use (or non-use) of the language of the colonial power, and the cultural and literary associations attached to that language

rhetoric originally, the art of speaking (and writing) effectively so as to persuade an audience; the term is now often used to cover the whole range of literary and linguistic devices

semiotics Swiss linguist Ferdinand Saussure (1857–1913) proposed that language is made up of a system of signs, which stand for something else, e.g. the word 'chair' stands more the 'thing we sit on'. His ideas led to the development of semiotics, which examines signs in such fields as literary theory, psychology and anthropology

simile a species of figurative writing involving a direct comparison of one thing to another. Similes typically make use of the words 'like' or 'as'

soliloquy a dramatic convention in which a character speaks directly to the audience, as if thinking aloud about motives, feelings and decisions

symbolism the use of symbols in a work of literature. A symbol is something which represents something else (often an idea or quality) by analogy or association – a writer may use conventional symbols, which form part of a literary or cultural tradition, as well as creating new ones

synecdoche a figure of speech in which a part is used to describe the whole, for example when describing a herd of cattle as 'one hundred head'

syntax the grammatical way in which words combine to create meaning

tenor and **vehicle** the two components of a **metaphor** (or **simile**): the tenor is the subject, and the vehicle the thing itself. For example, if Satan is described as being like a whale, Satan is the vehicle and the whale is the tenor

Geoff Ridden has worked in higher education for more than thirty years, publishing a substantial number of articles, including regular contributions to the *Milton Quarterly*. His books include *Studying Milton* and *Freedom and the English Revolution*. For most of his working life, he taught at King Alfred's University College, Winchester (now the University of Winchester), where he was Associate Dean in the Faculty of Arts until his retirement in 2008. He is now based in Ashland, Oregon, USA.

NOTES

NOTES

GCSE

Maya Angelou
I Know Why the Caged Bird Sings

Jane Austen
Pride and Prejudice

Alan Ayckbourn
Absent Friends

Elizabeth Barrett Browning
Selected Poems

Robert Bolt
A Man for All Seasons

Harold Brighouse
Hobson's Choice

Charlotte Brontë
Jane Eyre

Emily Brontë
Wuthering Heights

Brian Clark
Whose Life is it Anyway?

Robert Cormier
Heroes

Shelagh Delaney
A Taste of Honey

Charles Dickens
David Copperfield
Great Expectations
Hard Times
Oliver Twist
Selected Stories

Roddy Doyle
Paddy Clarke Ha Ha Ha

George Eliot
Silas Marner
The Mill on the Floss

Anne Frank
The Diary of a Young Girl

William Golding
Lord of the Flies

Oliver Goldsmith
She Stoops to Conquer

Willis Hall
The Long and the Short and the Tall

Thomas Hardy
Far from the Madding Crowd
The Mayor of Casterbridge
Tess of the d'Urbervilles
The Withered Arm and other Wessex Tales

L. P. Hartley
The Go-Between

Seamus Heaney
Selected Poems

Susan Hill
I'm the King of the Castle

Barry Hines
A Kestrel for a Knave

Louise Lawrence
Children of the Dust

Harper Lee
To Kill a Mockingbird

Laurie Lee
Cider with Rosie

Arthur Miller
The Crucible
A View from the Bridge

Robert O'Brien
Z for Zachariah

Frank O'Connor
My Oedipus Complex and Other Stories

George Orwell
Animal Farm

J. B. Priestley
An Inspector Calls
When We Are Married

Willy Russell
Educating Rita
Our Day Out

J. D. Salinger
The Catcher in the Rye

William Shakespeare
Henry IV Part I
Henry V
Julius Caesar
Macbeth
The Merchant of Venice
A Midsummer Night's Dream
Much Ado About Nothing
Romeo and Juliet
The Tempest
Twelfth Night

George Bernard Shaw
Pygmalion

Mary Shelley
Frankenstein

R. C. Sherriff
Journey's End

Rukshana Smith
Salt on the Snow

John Steinbeck
Of Mice and Men

Robert Louis Stevenson
Dr Jekyll and Mr Hyde

Jonathan Swift
Gulliver's Travels

Robert Swindells
Daz 4 Zoe

Mildred D. Taylor
Roll of Thunder, Hear My Cry

Mark Twain
Huckleberry Finn

James Watson
Talking in Whispers

Edith Wharton
Ethan Frome

William Wordsworth
Selected Poems

A Choice of Poets

Mystery Stories of the Nineteenth Century including The Signalman

Nineteenth Century Short Stories

Poetry of the First World War

Six Women Poets

For the AQA Anthology:
Duffy and Armitage & Pre-1914 Poetry
Heaney and Clarke & Pre-1914 Poetry
Poems from Different Cultures

Key Stage 3

William Shakespeare
Much Ado About Nothing
Richard III
The Tempest

Margaret Atwood
Cat's Eye
The Handmaid's Tale

Jane Austen
Emma
Mansfield Park
Persuasion
Pride and Prejudice
Sense and Sensibility

Pat Barker
Regeneration

William Blake
Songs of Innocence and of Experience

The Brontës
Selected Poems

Charlotte Brontë
Jane Eyre
Villette

Emily Brontë
Wuthering Heights

Angela Carter
The Bloody Chamber
Nights at the Circus
Wise Children

Geoffrey Chaucer
The Franklin's Prologue and Tale
The Merchant's Prologue and Tale
The Miller's Prologue and Tale
The Prologue to the Canterbury Tales
The Pardoner's Tale
The Wife of Bath's Prologue and Tale

Caryl Churchill
Top Girls

John Clare
Selected Poems

Joseph Conrad
Heart of Darkness

Charles Dickens
Bleak House
Great Expectations
Hard Times

John Donne
Selected Poems

Carol Ann Duffy
Selected Poems
The World's Wife

George Eliot
Middlemarch
The Mill on the Floss

T. S. Eliot
Selected Poems
The Waste Land

Sebastian Faulks
Birdsong

F. Scott Fitzgerald
The Great Gatsby

John Ford
'Tis Pity She's a Whore

John Fowles
The French Lieutenant's Woman

Michael Frayn
Spies

Charles Frazier
Cold Mountain

Brian Friel
Making History
Translations

William Golding
The Spire

Thomas Hardy
Jude the Obscure
The Mayor of Casterbridge
The Return of the Native
Selected Poems
Tess of the d'Urbervilles

Nathaniel Hawthorne
The Scarlet Letter

Seamus Heaney
Selected Poems from 'Opened Ground'

Homer
The Iliad
The Odyssey

Khaled Hosseini
The Kite Runner

Aldous Huxley
Brave New World

Henrik Ibsen
A Doll's House

James Joyce
Dubliners

John Keats
Selected Poems

Philip Larkin
High Windows
The Whitsun Weddings and Selected Poems

Ian McEwan
Atonement

Christopher Marlowe
Doctor Faustus
Edward II

Arthur Miller
All My Sons
Death of a Salesman

John Milton
Paradise Lost Books I and II

George Orwell
Nineteen Eighty-Four

Sylvia Plath
Selected Poems

William Shakespeare
Antony and Cleopatra
As You Like It
Hamlet
Henry IV Part I
King Lear
Macbeth
Measure for Measure
The Merchant of Venice
A Midsummer Night's Dream
Much Ado About Nothing
Othello
Richard II
Richard III
Romeo and Juliet
The Taming of the Shrew
The Tempest
Twelfth Night
The Winter's Tale

Mary Shelley
Frankenstein

Richard Brinsley Sheridan
The School for Scandal

Bram Stoker
Dracula

Alfred Tennyson
Selected Poems

Virgil
The Aeneid

Alice Walker
The Color Purple

John Webster
The Duchess of Malfi
The White Devil

Oscar Wilde
The Importance of Being Earnest
The Picture of Dorian Gray
A Woman of No Importance

Tennessee Williams
Cat on a Hot Tin Roof
The Glass Menagerie
A Streetcar Named Desire

Jeanette Winterson
Oranges Are Not the Only Fruit

Virginia Woolf
To the Lighthouse

William Wordsworth
The Prelude and Selected Poems

Wordsworth and Coleridge
Lyrical Ballads

Poetry of the First World War